HANDMADE LAMPSHADES

BEAUTIFUL DESIGNS TO ILLUMINATE YOUR HOME

BEAUTIFUL DESIGNS TO ILLUMINATE YOUR HOME

HANDMADE
LAMPSHADES

NATALIA PRICE-CABRERA

First published 2015 by
Guild of Master Craftsman Publications Ltd
Castle Place, 166 High Street, Lewes,
East Sussex BN7 1XU

ISBN 978 1 78494 069 0

A catalogue record for this book is available from
the British Library.

Publisher Jonathan Bailey
Production Manager Jim Bulley
Senior Project Editor Dominique Page
Editor Jason Hook
Managing Art Editor Gilda Pacitti
Designer Kate Haynes
Photographer Chris Gatcum

Set in Josefin Slab

Colour origination by GMC Reprographics

Printed and bound in China

CONTENTS

Chapter 2:
THE LAMPSHADE WORKSHOP

Chapter 3:
LEADING LIGHTS

'Lighting is the unsung hero of design.'
JONATHAN ADLER

INTRODUCTION

I have always loved lighting and what it can achieve in any space. With a little thought, lighting can elevate a space from a square soulless box to a place you really want to spend time in. And isn't that the essence of every home? That's certainly my belief. It was while trying to create a home that I wanted to spend time in that I discovered the art of lampshade making.

During my last big house move, I experienced what I call my lampshade epiphany. I had a very specific lampshade in mind for my living room, and had a complete vision of it in my head. Through extensive research I found something very similar, but it wasn't quite right and the price tag attached was completely outside of my budget. I will let you into a secret that even my partner doesn't know about: I so nearly bought it, until a little voice in my head told me to try and make one myself. I dismissed this voice for a few days, until I was at the rubbish tip and found an undamaged, but rather sad-looking, Empire lampshade. It cost the same as a cup of coffee, and it is the best money I have ever spent.

It was the beginning of an amazing journey that I am still on. Armed with that shade, I started to do some research into how to 'make a lampshade'. I found bits and pieces on the internet, but it was all very rudimentary and lacking in brio. I also trawled through what was available at that time in book form. I ordered the top four books on lampshade making, and frankly could have cried when I received them. I have worked in design- and photography-related book publishing for almost two decades and I know a beautiful book when I see one. These books were not beautiful. Yet lighting and lampshades are things of beauty in my eyes.

Not only did the books fail aesthetically, but the practical information left a lot to be desired. Out of the four, the two that were most useful were written around the 1950s. They presented very little visual information, but at least the text made sense and told me how to make a soft-sided fabric lampshade, which is what I wanted to know.

So, armed with my cheap frame and my 1950s instructional text I set about experimenting. And you know what? I fell in love. The whole process had me hooked. I wasn't sure if I was doing it 'right', but the result was exactly what I was originally looking for. And I haven't looked back since.

This book is a celebration of the lampshade. Lampshades really are a thing of beauty. They come in all shapes and sizes, and can be made from all manner of materials. We are going to concentrate on the art of making lampshades using fabric that is stretched in various ways over a wire lampshade frame. It doesn't have to cost the earth, quite the opposite – most of my lampshades are reuse projects. I love the idea of taking a tatty vintage lampshade and injecting new life into it. In this age of mass-produced, cheap lampshades, it's a breath of fresh air to be able to create something for the home that is unique, personal and doesn't break the bank.

I hope you enjoy immersing yourself in this book as much as I have enjoyed writing it. We start with a potted history of the lampshade, before moving on to invaluable information about the anatomy of the lampshade; fixtures and fittings; and types of lighting. There is a chapter dedicated to the basic generic techniques of lampshade making – such as the tools you need, fabrics and trims, binding a frame and safety issues – and after this we look at 16 step-by-step tutorials in the workshop section. To illustrate the dizzy heights lampshade making can reach there is a treat of a chapter lit up with inspirational images, tips and ideas from some of today's leading lampshade designers and makers. And at the end of the book there is a hugely useful Resources section and a visual feast for the eyes: two pages of nothing but beautiful lampshades. Read on, and let your imagination run wild.

A LITTLE LAMPSHADE HISTORY

The history of how we light our homes offers a fascinating insight into the ways in which we have lived, as well as how tastes in interior design have evolved. For many years, once the sun had set, candles and oil lamps were the only way to bring light into the home. Lampshades did exist, but they were predominantly of glass because of the dangers of exposing fabric shades to a naked flame. After a glass tube was invented to contain the flame, fabric lampshades became more commonplace.

Gas lighting was introduced early in the nineteenth century, producing a brilliant-white, intense and adjustable flame. It was also too bright for the eyes, so the lampshade became a necessity. Initially, the glass shade was most popular, but with time what we today recognize as the fabric lampshade – fabric stretched over a wire frame – developed, and soon the silk lampshade was ubiquitous in the home.

In the late 1870s, the invention of the incandescent filament electric light bulb transformed domestic lighting. With no flame or trace of combustion, all risk of intoxication, explosion or fire was removed. The previously utilitarian lampshade was set free. While its main function remained the tempering of the harsh light that emanated from early light bulbs, it could perform this role now with great pomp and ceremony. The age of the Victorian lampshade had arrived.

Early decorative shades were incredibly ornate. Primarily made of fabric, lace, flounces and frills, they tended to be modelled on dress and hat fashions. They were often so elaborate that little light could penetrate the shade, so interiors felt quite gloomy. Lampshades also became home to the household spider, so much so that nets called 'spider screens' were invented. With more people able to afford lighting in all of their rooms, and with a growing desire to create a welcoming and homely atmosphere, the lampshade as an aesthetic and decorative accessory came into its own. The craft of designing shades became an art, and lamp manufacturers started to take note. To this day, the elegant design of the traditional Victorian lampshade remains popular and there are many imitations available.

Around 1895, American artist and designer Louis Comfort Tiffany began producing stained-glass lampshades in elaborate patterns. The Tiffany lampshade was born. The style – a mosaic of brightly coloured glass – was highly distinctive. Some of the most famous Art Nouveau lamps were designed by Tiffany Studios. Originally conceived by designer Clara Driscoll, the Dragonfly lampshade is possibly Tiffany's most famous, featuring minuscule glass pieces in each detailed wing. The Tiffany lamp is still popular today, synonymous with elegance.

Edwardian fabric shades were as ornate as their Victorian predecessors, but lace and frills were replaced with beads and silk fringing. Frame shapes continued to be intricate and multi-panelled. In the mid-1920s, the clean lines of Art Deco became fashionable. Czech craftsmen created multi-coloured glass shades in globes, tulips and pointed stars. Elsewhere, lampshades were designed to imitate the styles of flapper dresses, with long silk sheaths ending in loose fringe or detailed fabric borders. By the 1930s, asymmetry in the lampshade was being introduced, and this period saw the development of the fabric sunburst shade.

After the Second World War, during rationing, lampshades were made from the available materials. These included parachute silk and even repurposed clothes. Pleating became very popular. In the following decades, lampshade design reflected the geometric forms of mid-century modernism. Ornamentation was replaced by pure shapes, such as stacked pyramids or huge cylindrical drums, in materials such as textured fibreglass, bamboo, bark cloth and woven raffia. In *Brilliant Lights & Lighting* (V&A Publications, 2004), Jane Pavitt writes: 'Clearly, the decorative light or lampshade did not fit a modernist philosophy of design – it was too whimsical, fashionable, feminine and homely to be regarded as "good design".'

In the 1970s, the famous Mop Cap was introduced, and there was a resurgence of the Tiffany dome pendant. The late 1970s and 1980s was the Laura Ashley era, which meant integrated interior schemes where lampshades matched curtains, sofa covers and cushions, all finished off with a proliferation of frills and ruffles. As a reaction to this overabundance of frothy nostalgia and frou frou, the 1990s were all about clean lines and minimal fuss. The drum lampshade had its heyday.

Since the turn of the century there has been a definite move towards historical frame shapes, reinterpreted in a contemporary way. In addition, the maker movement has exploded, perhaps encouraged by the make-do-and-mend trend. Modern lampshades are made from fabric, plastic, metal, wood and glass, and in many cases have become more art piece than mere shade. Designers working with lighting are constantly pushing the boundaries of available technologies and materials. These are exciting times. I urge you to further investigate the work of designers such as Gitta Gschwendtner (Corner Lamp and Up-The-Wall Lamp, 2002), Ingo Maurer, Esther van Groeningen (Segomil Lamp, 1999), Marc Newson, Ron Arad, Front (Animal Lamps, 2006), Tom Dixon (Etch, 2010), Troika (Circles and Countercircles, 2012), Bertjan Pot, Philippe Starck, Inga Sempé (Pleated Lamp, 2002), Omer Arbel (28 series, 2009), Jurgen Bey, Stuart Haygarth (Tide, 2004), Winnie Lui (White Chandelier), Nicolette Brunklaus (Hidden Royalty), Luc Merx (Fall of the Damned, 2007), Geoffrey Mann (Attracted to Light, 2005), Todd Boontje (Garland, 2002), Marcel Wanders and Ferruccio Laviani.

FACING PAGE, LEFT TO RIGHT:

A typical Victorian lampshade.
The Dragonfly lampshade made famous by Tiffany Studios.
Contemporary lampshades based on styles that were popular in the late 1800s and early 1900s.
Courtesy of Michelle Tomlinson, Shadez of Michelle, www.shadezofmichelle.com

ABOVE, LEFT TO RIGHT:

Lighting in the reception of hotel Andaz in the Netherlands by Marcel Wanders.
Zettel'z 5 by Ingo Maurer.

'No-one lights a lamp in order to hide it behind the door: the purpose of light is to create more light, to open people's eyes, to reveal the marvels around.'

PAULO COELHO

THE SECRET LIFE OF A LAMPSHADE

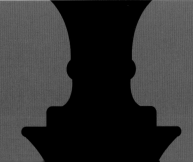

Before you begin making and creating, you need to know a little about the basics of a lampshade. It really is worth reading this chapter as it will help to create a foundation on which you can build your skills. It may not be as glamorous as some other parts of the book, but it is fundamental to your understanding of lampshade making and will help you to get the projects right.

This chapter will demystify some of the terms attached to lampshade making. It will introduce you to the anatomy of an individual frame, and it will show you the vast array of frames available to work with. The potential really is endless.

You will learn the technical stuff about fittings and fixtures, together with important guidelines. There is also information about types of lighting and function.

It won't take you long to read, and you will discover all the valuable advice you need to get going with the creative stuff.

Lampshade frames come in all shapes and sizes. The range of options is vast. You can even commission a frame maker to create a bespoke shade if you have trouble finding exactly what you are looking for (details can be found in the Resources section, *see page 187*).

TYPES OF FRAME

These are some of the generic shapes, explained.

DRUM
A cylindrical shade that resembles a drum. This is usually made from laminated PVC, with a top and bottom ring. It can also be made on a fixed frame and stitched.

COOLIE
A tapered, cone-shaped shade. There will be a marked difference between the top and bottom ring diameters. It is usually made from laminated PVC, with a top and bottom ring. It can also be made on a fixed frame and stitched.

EMPIRE
This sloping, fixed frame is narrow at the top and wider at the bottom. This type is probably the most common shape when it comes to making fabric-covered shades. It can work for a pendant or standing lamp.

TIFFANY
This frame shape is fairly elaborate and has a convex outer curve. It tends also to kick in at the bottom, which differentiates it from the bell shape.

BELL
This fixed frame resembles a bell, hence the name, and flares out at the bottom. Narrow at the top and wider at the bottom, bell-shaped shades are very versatile. They can be used as ceiling pendants, or as table and floor lamps.

SQUARE
A square or rectangle frame can come with straight or rounded corners. It can even have cut or inverted cut corners.

On the opposite page is a selection of frame shapes to whet your appetite. Some are more elaborate than others and, as such, will prove more time consuming and complicated to cover. However, the techniques presented in this book will equip you sufficiently to tackle any of these frame shapes. So, be bold and adventurous.

Single-scalloped
Empire

Retro reverse,
double-scalloped or
gallery-bottomed

Bell

Scalloped bottleneck

Square-waisted
or square pagoda

Collared, straight
Empire

Rectangular pagoda

Straight-edged
Empire

Reverse-scalloped or
Tiffany inverted

Bowed Empire
with Regency or
Clover bottom

Tapered drum

Tiffany plain,
half-bowl or dome

Double-scalloped
Empire

Cottage loaf or
Tiffany crown

Tiffany scallop

Bowed Empire
candle or
waisted frame

Hexagonal candle

Cottage loaf
or Tiffany
crown candle

Drum top and
bottom ring

Coolie top and
bottom ring with
duplex fitting

A fixed frame is made up of top and bottom rings (always called rings, regardless of their shape); side struts, staves or arms; and at least two gimbals, which have the fitting attached to them. Laminated PVC lampshades will only have a top and bottom frame; two gimbals minimum; and a fitting.

THE ANATOMY OF A LAMPSHADE

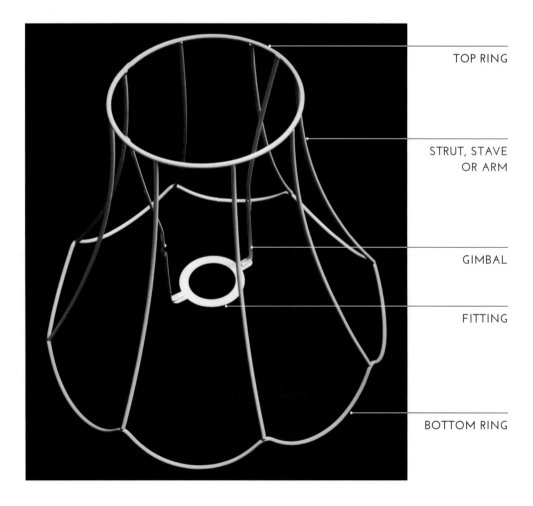

TOP RING

STRUT, STAVE OR ARM

GIMBAL

FITTING

BOTTOM RING

FIXTURES & FITTINGS

The fitting of a frame is the part that attaches to the light source, regardless of whether it is a lamp base or a pendant fitting. On the following pages are some of the most common fittings you will come across.

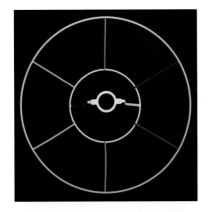
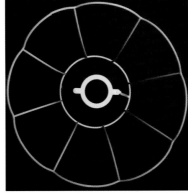
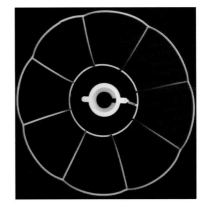

ABOVE & LEFT *The standard British fitting is ⁷⁄₈in (22mm) diameter (far left). The standard North American and continental European ES (Edison Screw) fitting is ¹¹⁄₁₆in (27mm) diameter (centre). A plastic converter called a 'boomerang' can be fitted into a larger ES fitting to reduce the size of the fitting to 22mm (left and above left). It makes sense to use ES fittings and provide a plastic converter as this means it can be fitted on to both lamp bases.*

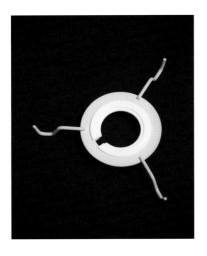

LEFT & FAR LEFT *A spider is an attachment that can be fitted to a duplex fitting, to enable the shade to be hung from the ceiling.*

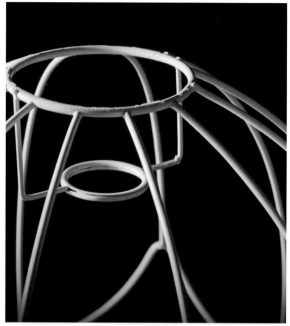

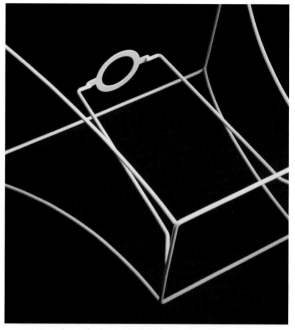

ABOVE *Pendant fitting. This shade can only be suspended from the ceiling.*

ABOVE *Fixed gimbal on a table lamp fitting.*

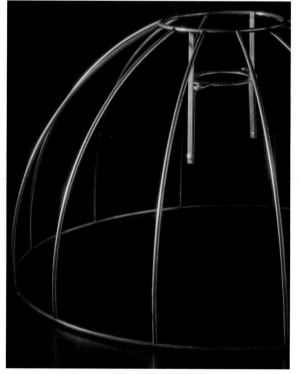

ABOVE & RIGHT *A reversible gimbal allows you to change a fitting from a pendant shade to a table shade. It can also be used at an angle so you can direct the lamp. The frame shown here is uncoated.*

ABOVE *A duplex fitting is a larger 4¹⁄₃in (110mm) fitting and is usually found on large standard lamp frames.*

ABOVE *Some frames come with a fixed spider.*

ABOVE *A butterfly clip is found on small candle frames for use on chandeliers and wall sconces; it simply clips on to the bulb.*

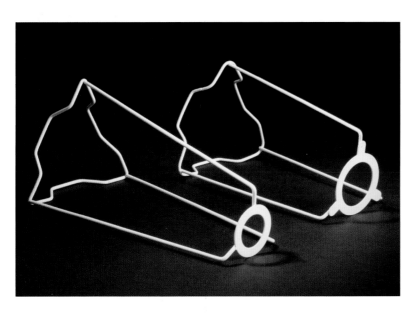

LEFT *Carriers support a duplex fitting on a standard lamp base and come in different sizes. To determine the size you need, measure the height of the frame from duplex fitting to bottom ring (see page 37), then deduct 2in (5cm) from this, and you should arrive at the carrier height required.*

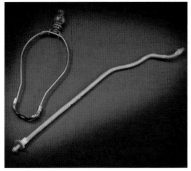

ABOVE & RIGHT *More commonly found in the USA, the harp is a small fitting that attaches to a harp carrier and is secured in place with a finial.*

ABOVE *Cables come in all sorts of wonderful colours these days.*

Your choice of frame shape and fabric covering will be informed by the end function of the lampshade and the effect you wish to create with it. There are four main types of lighting, which are discussed in more detail below. The lampshades in this book are predominantly for ambient and decorative lighting.

TYPES OF LIGHTING

Here is a brief outline of the role of lighting within the modern home.

AMBIENT LIGHTING
This is the background lighting that you find in pretty much every room in a home. It tends to make a space feel cosy if used successfully, due to its diffused nature.

ACCENT LIGHTING
This type of lighting allows you to highlight and draw attention to specific areas or objects within a room. Lighting fitted above pictures on the wall, or a lamp situated on a sideboard to lead the eye to a collection of ornaments, are examples of accent lighting.

TASK LIGHTING
As the name suggests, this type of lighting makes carrying out tasks easier. It tends to be directional, without a great deal of diffusion. Examples include desk lighting, bathroom lighting over a mirror, and light fittings found in kitchens.

DECORATIVE LIGHTING
Decorative lighting is more of a statement than a source of light, and serves little purpose other than to look beautiful.

RIGHT *A reading light can be classed as task lighting.*

ABOVE *Accent lighting is a fantastic way of drawing attention to a vignette of treasured objects.*

ABOVE LEFT *Ambient light on the landing, courtesy of the timeless Norm 69.*

LEFT *Decorative fairy lights add a little bit of magic to a child's dressing table.*

THE LAMPSHADE WORKSHOP

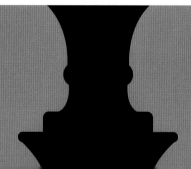

All you need to set up your lampshade workshop at home is a dedicated workspace. This can be a whole room, if you are lucky, or a section of a room. You could even transform a cupboard space into a nifty pull-out workroom. Storage and organization are key, as you will no doubt have a growing collection of fabrics, frames, ribbons, trims, threads, needles, pins, glue and reference material. Good lighting, a large, flat worktop, a sewing machine, comfortable seating, access to an iron and ironing board and some music will all help create a functional work environment.

This chapter is the real meat of the book. You will learn all about the tools you need; fabric qualities and types of trim; basic techniques of lampshade making; plus 16 step-by-step tutorials leading you through the different processes you can apply to making lampshades, including one on lamp bases. By the end of the chapter, you should be thoroughly equipped to tackle a whole range of techniques. Go forth and make lampshades! And when your friends ask you where you bought your beautiful lampshade, you can say with great delight and pride: 'I made it.'

The beauty of making lampshades is that you don't have to spend a lot of money on tools. You really can set yourself up in your workroom on a budget. Shop around to find good deals. You will probably already own a lot of the tools you need; it's just a matter of bringing them altogether to create a 'kitbox' of sorts.

TOOLS

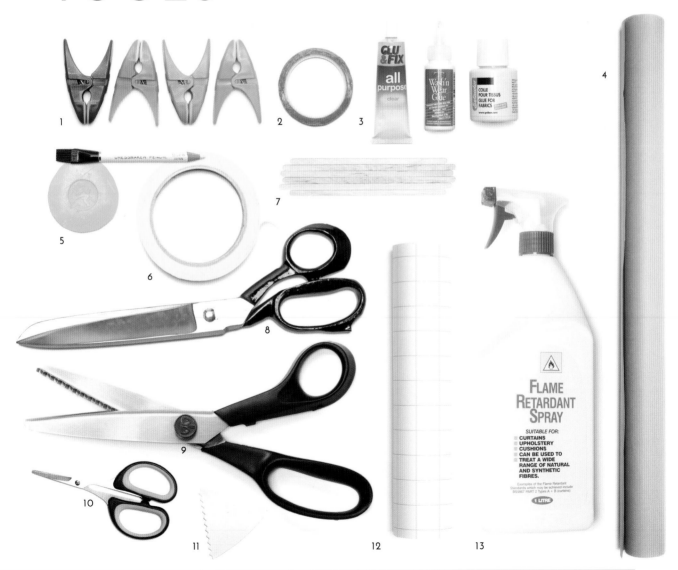

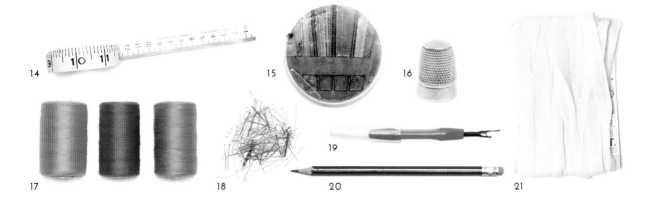

1. *Pegs.* It is worth investing in some good flathead pegs. They should have a solid spring mechanism and a firm grip. Plastic ones wipe clean and don't create indentations in the fabric. Pegs are invaluable when it comes to pegging out your fabric.

2. *Double-sided sticky tape.* Crucial for making drum lampshades and any shade involving coated PVC.

3. *Fabric glue.* There are lots, so experiment until you find the one that best works for you.

4. *Brown paper.* Used to create panel templates. Best bought as a roll and not folded.

5. *Tailor's chalk.* This comes in many forms. I prefer the tablets, but you can also get it in pencil form with a brush attached to rub it off the fabric.

6. *Masking tape.* Used to hold down fabric when you are making a drum lampshade.

7. *Wooden stirrers.* Perfect for applying glue.

8. *Large fabric scissors.* Keep these sharp. They're great for cutting lengths of fabric.

9. *Pinking shears.* These have sawtoothed blades instead of conventional straight blades. They create a zigzag pattern when you cut fabric, and minimize frayed edges.

10. *Small embroidery scissors.* Used to get in close and perform delicate cutting procedures.

11. *Rolled-edge serrated tool.* You need one of these to make any drum-shaped shade. Alternatively, you can use an old store card.

12. *Self-adhesive lampshade PVC.* Strong, UV stable, flame retardant, antistatic, and engineered for lampshade making.

13. *Flame retardant spray.* To make your lampshades safe, you must invest in this.

14. *Tape measure.* You will need to measure a lot, so get one of these. A conventional ruler just won't do the job.

15. *Needles.* A variety of sizes is always useful, as is a curved needle. 'Inbetweens' are the best for sewing fabric to the binding frame as they are short and sturdy, so less likely to snap.

16. *Thimble.* This is a must if you want to hand stitch fabric to your frame. Without it, you'll end up with very sore fingers indeed.

17. *Thread.* 'Bold' thread is a very strong thread, which is ideal for stitching fabric to the frame. If you can't get hold of bold thread, then use polyester thread doubled up. It's much stronger than silk or cotton thread.

18. *Pins.* To make lampshades, you will need pins and lots of them. 'Lills' or sequin pins are ideal for pinning fabric to your frame. Lills are shorter than regular dressmaking pins, so you should in theory stab yourself less often! Dressmaking pins will be useful for everything else. Always avoid bent pins!

19. *Unpicking tool.* We all make mistakes, so it's always handy to have something with which to unpick unwanted stitches.

20. *Soft-leaded pencil.* Used to mark fabric when tailor's chalk doesn't show up for whatever reason.

21. *Binding tape.* Used to bind the frame. *See page 32* for more on this.

There is a plethora of fabrics out there, just waiting to be manipulated over a lampshade frame. In my workroom, I have a large open shelving unit onto which I stack my fabrics by colour so I can instantly see how fabrics might work together. On the following pages are a few of my favourites. This is not a comprehensive overview by any means. It will, however, equip you with a foundation on which to build your resource.

FABRICS

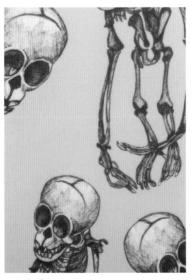

Peach skin
This is a highly malleable and stretchy fabric that has the texture of peach skin. It has a tendency to pick up fluff and stray threads, but these can be easily removed with a scrunched-up bit of masking tape (sticky side out). The fabric shown here was designed by Stephanie Chadwick.

Digitally printed silk
This is a beautiful fabric to work with. The gorgeous design shown here is by Nicola Adams, an extremely talented surface pattern designer.

ABOVE *The Susana shade (Mols & Tati-Lois) is made using a mixture of contemporary upholstery fabrics, vintage French fabrics and even some vintage Laura Ashley designs.*

TIP
Always consider the function of your fabric. It is a good idea to hold it up to the light before committing to it, as light affects fabric in different ways and can change the perceived colour.

Cotton
This is one of my favourite fabrics. Lightweight cotton laminates very well, so consider it if you are making a drum or a coolie lampshade.

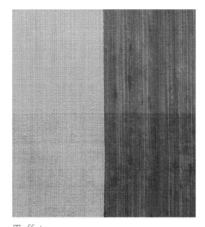

Taffeta
This is a crisp, smooth, plain woven fabric that is made from silk or rayon. The word is Persian in origin, and means 'twisted woven'. Taffeta is considered a high-end fabric. It is fairly robust, so I would recommend hand stitching.

Upholstery fabrics
Although these can often be fairly heavyweight, you can create some incredibly striking lampshades using upholstery fabrics. For an example, look at the Susana shade (on the facing page).

Bark cloth
This cloth was originally made by pummelling sodden lengths of the inner bark of the *Moraceae* tree family into sheets. Today, 'bark cloth' tends to refer to a double-weave, cotton-based, densely woven, textured fabric. The versatile cloth is synonymous with home furnishings of the 1940s to 1960s. (*See page 166*, Folly & Glee.)

Linen
This is a natural fibre made from the flax plant. It is very strong, but tends to crease easily. It's not very flexible, so it's best used on drums. Linen has fantastic antistatic qualities, so it doesn't attract dust. Vintage linen can be wonderful when transformed into lampshades. It also takes dye fantastically well.

Silk scarves
You can pick up some truly stunning vintage silk scarves in charity shops for next to nothing. They can be used to create incredibly beautiful and individual lampshades. Either used as decoupage (*see page 114*) or in their entirety (*see page 72*), the silk scarf is a hugely versatile addition to your fabric stash.

Vintage fabrics
I am a huge fan of vintage fabrics. You can pretty much adapt any type of vintage fabric to lampshade making. Vintage linen, clothes, tea towels, scarves and even bedding can be transformed into a truly unique lampshade.

Shot silk
Silk creates an elegant and timeless finish. There are many types, but one of my favourites is shot silk. This is a silk woven from warp and weft yarns of two or more colours, creating an iridescent patina.

Tartan and tweed
Tartan is a pattern of criss-crossed horizontal and vertical bands in multiple colours. It originated in woven wool, but is now made in many materials. Tweed is a rough, unfinished woollen fabric in either plain or twill weave. It may have a check or herringbone pattern.

Batik
This fabric is dyed using a wax-resist process. The batik is made in two ways: by drawing dots and lines with the wax using a spouted tool called a canting; or by printing the resist with a copper stamp called a cap. The wax resists the dyes and is removed using boiling water.

Sari
The word *sari* is derived from Sanskrit and means 'strip of cloth'. I am a huge fan of vintage saris, not only because they are beautiful but because they are a great way to source a lot of fabric. On average, a sari can measure 16–26ft (5–8m) in length, and 2–4ft (60–120cm) in width.

Felt
Produced by matting and pressing fibres together, felt can be made from natural fibres such as wool, or synthetic fibres such as acrylic. It is incredibly versatile. A highly durable fabric that doesn't unravel, felt is very resistant to dirt. You can make felt by washing an old jumper on a very hot wash. (*See page 94* for an embellished felt dome project.)

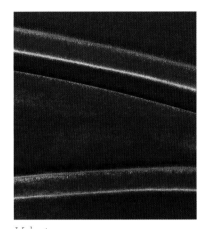

Velvet
A sumptuous material that just shouts luxury. Velvet is a woven, tufted fabric. The cut threads create a short pile. Depending upon the density and quality of the velvet, it can be incredibly malleable and works beautifully to cover a lampshade.

Brocade
The name comes from the Italian *broccato*, meaning 'embossed cloth'. Brocade can be quite a heavy fabric, but if used wisely it can look striking on a lampshade. You will probably have to hand stitch it.

Kimono
Kimonos were traditionally made from silk and satin. Vintage kimono fabric is beautiful and a treat to work with.

Sheer fabrics
Chiffon can be made from synthetic fibres, but cotton- or silk-based chiffons take dye more effectively. Chiffon is fairly transparent due to its mesh-like qualities. Organza, another sheer fabric, is a plain weave fabric traditionally made from silk. Today, it is more likely to be derived from a polyester or nylon base.

SAFETY

To make your lampshade safe to use, you will have to treat any fabric in your design with flame retardant spray prior to assembling the shade. You can purchase this from most fabric shops or online. I list a few options in the Resources section (*see page 187*). It is extremely important that you follow the manufacturer's guidelines exactly. The bottle should come with very clear instructions. I always work in a very well-ventilated space, usually outside, and I wear a dust mask to make sure that I don't inhale any of the spray. I highly recommend carrying out a patch test on your fabric prior to spraying it all, as some fabrics will run and as a result you could end up with a stack of material that's not usable. Always leave fabric to dry in a ventilated space, too, and do not use until completely dry. Once it is dry, you can iron treated fabric without any problems.

I treat all fabric used on soft-sided shades, be it the lining or the outer cover. I also treat the lining fabric on double-sided drums. You don't need to worry about single-sided drums, coolies, fairy lights, hard-sided pagodas or square-waisted shades as the self-adhesive PVC is already heatproof. For peace of mind I always recommend using a 60-watt bulb or less, and I always follow the rule never to have any part of the covered lampshade closer than 4in (10cm) to the light source. Halogen bulbs produce a lot of heat, so I would suggest you steer clear of those.

Always get light fittings professionally tested if you are selling on to other people. You don't want an electrical fault on your conscience. You can find out where to get this done by getting in touch with your local electrician or by visiting an electrical goods store. It isn't expensive at all.

To me, the trimmings section of any fabric shop is like a sweet shop. I adore trimmings and have a workroom full of them. I store them in see-through bags by colour and I keep embellishments in clear jars. This way I can pretty much tell at a glance what I have to hand. You can buy trimmings by the metre, on a roll or a mini-bolt. It's always a good idea to have a rummage in the off-cut baskets, too, as small, candle lampshades don't need a great deal of trim and you can often find some really good deals.

TRIMMINGS & EMBELLISHMENTS

If you are a bit of a magpie, like me, then you will regularly find vintage trims and ribbons in charity shops. You can discover some truly beautiful and unusual pieces, just waiting for a second spin on the dance floor. All they need is a wash and an iron. Be careful, as they may shrink and the colour might run. If they are fairly neutral in colour, you may even wish to dye them vibrant colours. The choice is yours.

Trimmings can be divided into the following categories:

RIBBON
Ribbon comes in all sizes and finishes. You might come across velvet, satin, gathered, wire-edged, lace, ruffles, Jacquard and metallic.

FRINGING
Used to trim the bottom ring of a lampshade, there are all sorts of different types of fringing, including: tasselled, beaded, pompoms or bobble fringing, bullion, feathers, loop fringe, knot fringe, and brush cut.

GIMP
This is a narrow, decorative trim traditionally made from cotton, silk or wool. It is sometimes stiffened with metallic wire or a thick cord running through it. Gimp is incredibly malleable, so it is great for trimming lampshades as you can work it around bends.

RIC RAC OR RICK RACK
A favourite in the 1970s, ric rac comes in a variety of sizes from jumbo to very small. It is instantly identifiable, due to its zigzag form, and it can be used to create a beautiful scalloped edge.

RIGHT *The world really is your oyster when it comes to embellishing your lampshades. You can use all sorts of things, such as beads, sequins, buttons, felt flowers, crocheted squares and appliquéd patches.*

DIY TRIMMINGS

You can also make your own trimmings. Popular ones include simple gathering, petal-edged ruching, shell edging, fly-stitch rouleau and box-pleated edges. There are many good and easy-to-follow tutorials online.

TIP

To stop trimmings unravelling when you cut them, put a piece of tape over each end until you need to sew or glue.

GROSGRAIN

This is a type of ribbon characterized by its ribbed form. It comes in varying widths and myriad colours.

BRAID

Braid is a woven trim involving three or more strands, which resembles macramé. There are many types of braid, with fantastic names such as Soutache, loop braid, and middy braid.

BIAS BINDING

Ready-made bias binding comes in an array of colours. However, if you fancy making your own there are hundreds of good online tutorials. Cut on the bias, it is perfect for lampshades as it goes around corners easily.

ABOVE *VV Rouleaux tassel fringing on the Candy Vamp lampshade (Mols & Tati-Lois).*

Before you start making lampshades, you need to become versed in the basic techniques. The following pages provide you with a solid foundation on which to build. We will look at best practice while making a lampshade; how to recondition a neglected charity-shop find; why we need to bind the frame and how to do this; what the streetly stitch entails; how to make balloon lining and then insert it; and, finally, how to make a gimbal tidy. It really is worth reading through this section before moving on to the tutorials.

BASIC TECHNIQUES

Try to remember the following while making your lampshade:

- Avoid using hand cream, as this will make your hands slippery and you may also transfer greasy marks on to the fabric you are using.
- Wash your hands regularly with cold water, as the heat of your hands can distort the shape of the fabric.
- Always carry and hold a frame by its gimbal if you can. Avoid touching the fabric as much as possible. If you must touch a lampshade, do so with the back of your hand as this emits less heat than the palm.
- Make sure your iron is clean. Any dirt will transfer straight to your fabric and could leave marks that just won't budge. Check your ironing board, too. Everything should be as clean as possible. This goes for your whole workspace.
- Lampshade making is hazardous and you will prick yourself repeatedly. Don't worry, though. If you get blood on your shade, take a scrap of the same fabric you are using and chew on it to soak it in your own saliva. Use this to dab at the blood spot, as the enzymes will help dilute the blood until it completely disappears. Trust me, it works!
- Always use a thimble. Your fingers will get very sore from inserting and pulling and pushing so many needles and pins.
- Use a hair dryer to get rid of loose threads and any other bits of debris your shade may have picked up. A small duster works well, too, as does masking tape scrunched into a ball, sticky side out.

BEWARE OF SELVEDGE
Selvedge is the edge of woven fabric finished in such a way as to prevent unravelling. It often has a narrow tape effect, different from the body of the fabric. Make sure you do not use this part of the fabric when creating your panels, as it will look noticeably different to the main body of the fabric.

STEAM POWER
It may seem obvious, but I cannot stress enough that all fabric used for lampshade making must be really well ironed to remove any creases prior to working with it. Even a faint crease could ruin the finished look. So, invest in a decent steam iron. It really is worth it.

RECONDITIONING A CHARITY SHOP FIND

In most cases you will probably buy a brand-new frame from a third-party manufacturer (there are some recommendations in the Resources section on page 187). However, if you are a junk shop junkie like me, then you will regularly come across second-hand shades that just need a little love and attention to restore them to their former glory or even elevate them far beyond. Just make sure that the frame isn't bent out of shape, as this will make it very hard to re-cover with any success.

A battered drum can be stripped easily. Discard the fabric and laminated PVC and just keep hold of the top and bottom rings. These can be cleaned using acetone. Lighter fluid is great for removing stubborn glue – but be sure to clean it off thoroughly afterwards. You may find a frame that needs nothing more than a little tidying up. This can be done easily using white nail polish. It ingeniously covers up any spot where the enamel that coats the frame might have been chipped away. For more dilapidated frames where the enamel is beyond repair, you will need to sand right back to the metal of the frame. The metal does need to be coated in some way, otherwise it can become rusty with the heat of the light bulb and will ruin any fabric covering you might have created. You can buy enamel paints (radiator enamel, for example) from your local hardware store with which to recoat the frame. If you want to be more adventurous, there are some amazing car spray paints that come in a huge range of colours. Be sure to always read the manufacturer's instructions, as you often have to apply primer beforehand. You can really make a feature of the frame in this way, particularly if the shade is going to be suspended overhead and the frame is on show.

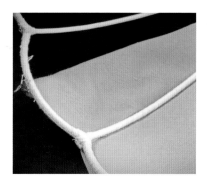

ABOVE *Sometimes you will find a second-hand lampshade that is actually in pretty good condition. Here, all that needed doing was to remove the fabric and stitches. The binding was still secure and there was no yellowing, so there was no need to rebind the frame.*

ABOVE *This is an example of a really battered frame. This will need sanding back to the original metal all over. It will then need recoating, with enamel paint or car paint.*

ABOVE *For small touch-up jobs you can use white nail polish. Apply several coats, allowing drying time in between.*

BINDING THE FRAME

Why do we need to bind the frame? In order to pin and sew on to a frame, there needs to be something to pin and sew into. This is the function of the binding. Without it, it would be nigh on impossible to stitch anything on to a frame. Binding tape today is a loose-weave cotton tape sometimes referred to as India tape. Historically, binding tape has gone by various other names: Prussian tape, Jap tape and Paris tape. You can also use traditional bias binding, which comes in a wide range of colours. Make sure you iron one side open, though, so that it doesn't become too bulky. Another alternative is to make your own bias binding from the same fabric as you are using to cover the shade, or a contrasting one depending on personal taste. There are literally thousands of online tutorials showing you how to make bias binding, so explore.

01

01 Measure the circumference of your top ring and then multiply by 2.5. This is the length of tape you will need to bind the top ring. Where a strut meets the top ring, create a little tail of tape.

02

02 Make a figure of eight with the tape around the join between the top ring and a strut. This will secure the start of your binding.

03

03 Carry on binding the tape around the top ring, making sure that you overlap the tape slightly each time you wind it around the ring. Create a figure of eight each time you come to a strut and where the gimbal meets the top ring. To finish off the top ring binding, hold the tape with a peg and then stitch as shown on page 34. Do the same for the bottom ring. In some cases you will only need to bind the top and bottom ring; for example when you are making a pleated or swathed lampshade. The binding should not move at all, as this is what you'll be stitching into when you attach the fabric.

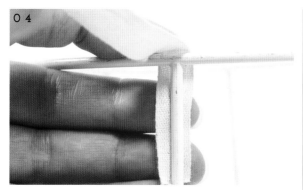

0 4 To bind a strut, measure tape out to 2.5 times the length of the strut. Create a little tail where the strut meets the top ring. You would usually have already bound your top ring before doing this; however, to make things clearer to see I have not bound the top ring for the purposes of this demonstration.

0 5 Holding the tail in place, wind the long length of tape around the tail and strut to secure it in place.

0 6 Working down the strut, overlap the tape diagonally. Be mean with the tape, so that the binding doesn't become too bulky.

0 7 When you arrive at the bottom of the strut (a), make a figure of eight with the tape where it meets the bottom ring (b).

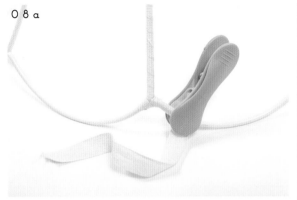

08a

09a

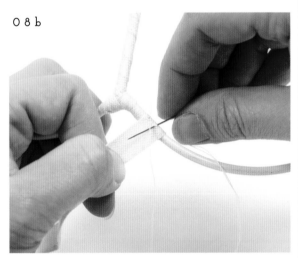

08b

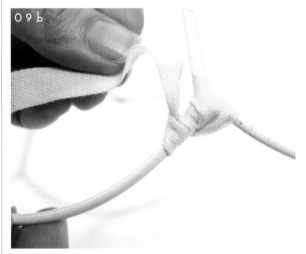

09b

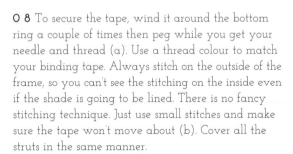

08 To secure the tape, wind it around the bottom ring a couple of times then peg while you get your needle and thread (a). Use a thread colour to match your binding tape. Always stitch on the outside of the frame, so you can't see the stitching on the inside even if the shade is going to be lined. There is no fancy stitching technique. Just use small stitches and make sure the tape won't move about (b). Cover all the struts in the same manner.

09 This is a temporary strut binding. You need this to create a balloon lining, and whenever you need to stretch fabric across half the frame. The Chandelier project (*see page 78*) uses this technique. Bind the strut as previously explained (a), but finish off with a knot instead of stitching so that the binding can be removed easily at a later date (b).

RIGHT *Binding tape comes in various colours and is usually available in two widths: ¼in (7mm) and ⅜in (1cm). I tend to use the wider tape, but the thinner tape is great for small candle frames.*

DYEING BINDING TAPE

India tape or cotton binding tape takes cold-water dye very well, so you can completely transform the look of binding tape from the mundane to something you really want to have on show. There is an amazing range of colours available and it's relatively cheap, particularly if you dye a big batch in one go. You can pick up dye very easily from your local hardware store or order it online. Dyeing binding tape is something you can do in an afternoon, then hang it out to dry on a radiator or over the bath for use the next day. This can eliminate the need for lining, depending on the final look you are going for. Note: Beware of shrinkage. If you have pre-measured the binding tape prior to dyeing, add an extra 4in (10cm) to be on the safe side.

STREETLY STITCH

Streetly stitch is a locking stitch used to secure fabric on to the lampshade frame, with the back stitch forming the actual locking stitch. It is a type of double stitch, which, if my sources are correct, has its roots in glove making. For the purposes of this demonstration, I am using black thread on white so that you can see the stitching clearly. In reality you would use a thread as close in colour to your fabric as possible, unless of course you want the stitching to be a feature and you plan not to hide it with trimmings. It is imperative that you catch both the fabric and the binding thread as you stitch. Floating stitches are of no use at all.

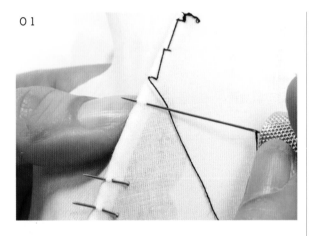

01 Here, I am stitching along a strut during the process of hand-stitching individual panels of fabric to the frame; but this is also the stitch you would use to secure fabric to the top and bottom rings. Feed the needle through the fabric and the binding tape, working from right to left and using a thimble. This will create your diagonal stitch. You are, in effect, creating a zigzag.

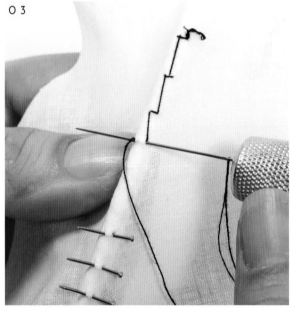

03 Take the stitch back on itself, effectively making a back stitch. This is your locking stitch.

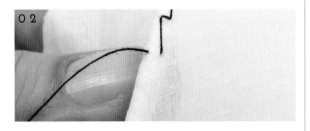

02 Pull the thread through on the left. Try to make sure the size and distance between stitches is as uniform as possible.

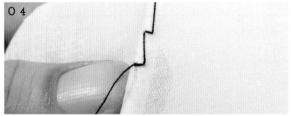

04 Pull the thread through. You are now ready to start again from Step 1 with a diagonal stitch.

MAKING THE LINING

The main purpose of a lining is to cover up your stitching and bound struts, especially in hanging shades. It is particularly relevant if you have embroidered or stitched into your outer cover in any way, as it will hide untidiness. You don't have to line a shade, it's down to end usage and personal taste. You might want the binding to be a feature, or you may be using a double-weave fabric such as bark cloth (*see page 25*); in which case the pattern is seen equally on the right and wrong side of the fabric, so lining is unnecessary. Lining also helps diffuse the light emitted from a light bulb. This is important if you are working with sheer fabrics. Aesthetically, the lining can also be decorative. You may have a pendant fitting over a dining area, which will be regularly viewed from below; in which case, a colourful lining would make a striking feature.

Traditionally, lining is made using jersey-based fabrics. However, I tend to use a lot of other types, depending on the overall scheme I have in mind. The fabric does need to have a degree of stretch to it, though, and you must always work on the bias. I will show you how to make a traditional balloon lining, and give a brief overview of other types of lining. Getting the lining right first time is an incredibly fiddly, and often frustrating, process. Persevere, as a good lining will give your lampshades a professional finish.

RIGHT *The Susana (Mols & Tati-Lois) is made from a collection of vintage French fabrics, with a Laura Ashley design as the lining. The lining can be as decorative as the outer cover. There are no hard and fast rules.*

MEASURING YOUR FRAME ACCURATELY

Place a tape measure or ruler across the bottom of the lampshade (not around it). Do the same across the top of the lampshade. This will give you the diameters of the top and bottom rings. To determine the circumference, simply multiply the diameter by 3.15. To measure the height, sit the lampshade on a flat surface; then, with the ruler on the inside of the lampshade, measure from the flat surface to the top.

CALCULATING THE AMOUNT OF LINING FABRIC

The amount of fabric you will need for your lining very much depends on the size of your frame. To make a rough calculation, measure the depth of your frame (from top ring to bottom ring) with a tape measure, making sure to include any curved edges. Add 4 3/4in (12cm) to this measurement. Next, measure half the circumference of the bottom ring and add 4 3/4in (12cm) here, too.

MAKING A TRADITIONAL BALLOON LINING

01

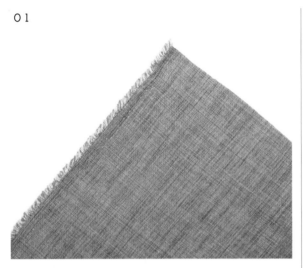

0 1 Take your chosen lining fabric and iron it. Make sure you are working on the bias. You should have what looks like a triangle. Cut to size (*see page 37*).

02

0 2 The frame must be permanently bound on the top and bottom rings; and either permanently bound on the struts, or temporarily bound on two of the struts sitting opposite each other (*see pages 32–35*), depending on the method you plan to use to cover the outside of your lampshade.

03

0 3 Drape the fabric right side down over half of your frame, making sure that you are working on the bias at all times. You should have sufficient fabric to be able to drape it from one bound strut to the bound strut sitting directly opposite.

04

0 4 Begin pinning, using lills at each of the four corners where top and bottom rings meet bound struts. Make sure the lills go through both fabric and binding tape, and always pin away from the frame to avoid making unnecessary holes in your lining. Add more lills evenly around the frame, stretching the fabric taut as you work your way around. Do not overstretch the lining, particularly if you are using jersey.

05 You should end up with a pin every ³⁄₈in (1cm) along the two struts and the top and bottom rings. Check how taut the stretched fabric is with the back of your hand. It should sound like a drum when tapped. If it doesn't, re-pin and stretch some more. This takes a while and you will encounter areas that pucker, so persevere. Slowly and carefully, you will be able to manipulate the fabric into place.

06 Once you are happy with your stretched fabric, take a soft pencil or some tailor's chalk and draw a line along each strut – adding ¼in (3cm) beyond each ring top and bottom. Try to stay as true to the edge of the strut as possible.

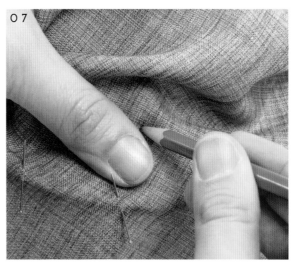

07 Working your way along top and bottom rings, make a hole where each remaining strut meets the top and bottom ring with the point of a pencil a thumb's length away from the ring. This will help you position the lining correctly when you come to insert it.

08 Remove all the pins and give your fabric an iron.

09 Place your lining template on top of a second piece of fabric with the grain running in the same direction. The fabrics should be right sides facing one another.

11 Machine stitch ⅛in (3mm) inside each chalk line, adding 2in (5cm) top and bottom of the lines. Turn the fabric around, and stitch over your first line of stitches. Now trim along each seam, leaving ¼in (5mm) seam allowance. Do not trim anything off the top and bottom of the lining. To secure the lining further, you could use an overlocker.

10 Pin the two pieces of fabric together along each line of tailor's chalk using dressmaking pins. Keep the fabric as flat as possible so you don't get any distortions in the shape of the lining.

12

12 Your lining is now ready to insert, but first you need to make the outer covering for your shade. So, put the lining to one side.

INSERTING THE LINING

01

01 Once you have finished your outer covering, you are ready to line your lampshade. If you have bound your side struts temporarily, you must remove the binding before you insert the lining. Always drop the lining in with the right side out and the seams in.

02

02 Line up each seam with a strut. Do not press the seams, or they will show up when the lampshade is illuminated.

03

03 Pin each seam to the bottom ring using lills. Pin away from the frame.

04

04 Work around the lining and line up each hole you made (in Step 7 on page 39) with each remaining strut.

0 5

0 5 Pin the lining to the bottom ring.

0 6

0 6 Work around the frame, pinning and stretching the lining fabric as you go. Once the bottom ring is pinned out, move on to the top ring.

0 7

0 7 To fit your lining properly, you will need to make a small incision in the fabric where it meets the gimbal. Cut in small increments so you don't cut too much. It's a bit of trial and error to begin with, but the aim is to be able to pull the fabric taut up to the top ring around the gimbals. It takes practice, but you will get the hang of it.

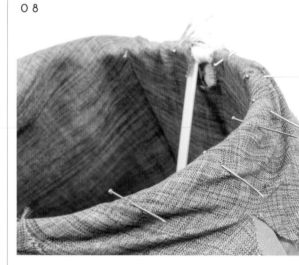

0 8

0 8 Once you have cut around the gimbal, you can start to stretch and pin the fabric to the top ring, working out any puckering or creases as you go.

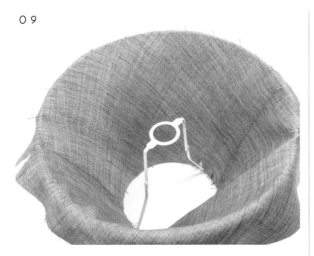

0 9 Here, you can see one half of the lining stretched and pinned in position, with the other half still to do. This is just to show you the difference between stretched and fitted lining and lining fabric that has yet to be manipulated in to place.

1 0 Once you have pinned out the whole of the top ring, and you are happy with the stretch of the lining, stitch the fabric to the top and bottom rings using the streetly stitch (*see page 36*). Here I am using white thread to show up, but in reality you would use thread to best match the colour of your fabric.

TIP

Before inserting your lining, always check for loose threads, fraying seams and untrimmed binding tape. Any stray fibres will really stand out once the shade is illuminated, and it will be too late to do anything about it without removing and refitting the lining – a lengthy and annoying process.

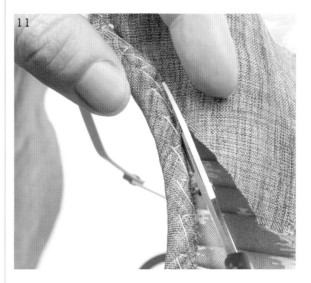

MATCHING THREADS

Always use a natural thread such as cotton with a fabric made from natural fibre, and a polyester thread when using polyester-based fabrics. They will have the same 'give' in them.

1 1 Trim off all excess fabric close to your stitching. Make sure you do not cut into the stitching by mistake, as this will affect the stretch and you could end up with baggy lining. To finish off, add gimbal tidies (*see page 45*).

OTHER TYPES OF LINING

There are several other ways you can line a lampshade. You can sew panels on to the outside of your frame before stitching the outer cover on, or at the same time. This is called an exterior lining, and will mean that your binding is on view. Examples of this can be found in Club Tartan (*see page 106*) and Lady Penelope (*see page 94*). This approach is often a necessity if you are working with an ornate frame. It is almost impossible to fit a balloon lining into some frame shapes.

You can also create a gathered lining. In essence, this is the same as making a pleated, external lampshade cover (as on Ikata on page 132) – but you make it on the inside of the frame, with the right side of the fabric facing out.

My favourite type of lining is the multi-panelled approach. This creates a balloon-lining effect, but allows you to work with slightly more awkward frame shapes. It also enables you to use a mix of

different fabric patterns, if you wish. This works beautifully for any type of suspended lampshade where the underside is what is most seen, and therefore the feature. To make this type of lining, just follow the steps on the Frida Rocks and Belle Trixie projects (*see page 88 and page 102*) to create a panelled 'skirt' – but, instead of using it as an outer cover, insert it as a lining, following the instructions on page 41 for inserting a balloon lining.

RIGHT *The Caliana Peacock lampshade (Mols & Tati-Lois) is lined using the multi-panelled method. I've also trimmed the underside with velvet ribbon.*

MAKING A GIMBAL TIDY

A gimbal tidy is a small piece of fabric used to conceal the raw and untidy edges of the lining fabric around the gimbal.

01

01 Measure out 4¾ x 2in (12 x 5cm), ideally in the same fabric as the lining. You need the same number of tidies as there are gimbals. In this case, there are two.

02

02 Cut out each 4¾ x 2in (12 x 5cm) piece of fabric.

03

03 Fold the raw edges in on themselves.

04

04 Pull the fabric so it becomes taut.

05

05 Fold the fabric strip in half again.

06

06 This shows the area we are going to conceal.

07

07 Thread the gimbal tidy under the gimbal, making sure the closed, folded edge is uppermost.

08

08 Position the gimbal tidy so that it covers all the cut fabric. Pull it tight, or it will flap about and could expose unsightly raw edges.

09

09 Pin the gimbal tidy in place.

10

10 Stitch the gimbal tidy using the streetly stitch, then trim off the two 'tails' of fabric to give you a neat finish. Now, you can add a trim.

FRAME TYPE: Drum lampshade (top and bottom rings with 3 gimbals and a fitting)

TECHNIQUE: Simple drum lampshade using self-adhesive lampshade PVC and double-sided tape

PROJECT TIME: 2 hours

SKILL LEVEL: 🔦🔦🔦🔦🔦

PIXIE FOLK

A MAGICAL FOREST FULL OF FANCIFUL CREATURES IN BOLD MONOCHROME

FABRIC & DECORATION

Papercut Forest Black from the Westex Collection/Japanese import, 40in (1m) width x 12in (30cm) drop

³/₈in (1cm) red velvet ribbon, 40in (1m) (optional)

red medium-sized pompoms, 40in (1m) (optional)

TOOLS & MATERIALS

- tape measure
- paper scissors
- self-adhesive lampshade PVC
- fabric scissors
- steam iron
- masking tape
- tailor's chalk or soft pencil
- small embroidery scissors
- double-sided tape
- rolled-edge serrated tool, or an old store card

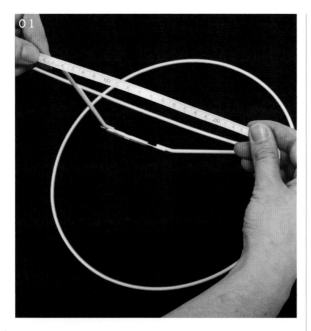

01 Determine the circumference of your rings by measuring them with a tape measure.

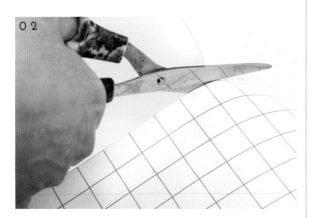

02 The height of your shade is variable, depending on taste and final use. Work out what you want and then cut out a piece of the self-adhesive lampshade PVC, using the dimensions you arrive at. The height will be the vertical measurement, while the circumference will represent the horizontal measurement. Add ³/4in (2cm) to the circumference measurement for the overlap. In this example, I have used the following measurements: 38in (97cm) for the length (circumference plus ³/4in [2cm]) and 8³/4in (22cm) for the height. The PVC comes with a grid on its reverse side to ensure you cut straight lines.

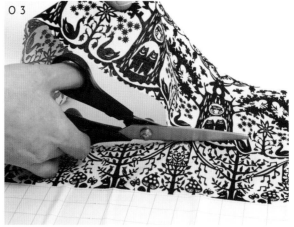

03 Position your fabric flat face up on a large work surface, then lay the PVC on top of it. Cut your fabric out to create a workable template. Leave at least 4in (10cm) all the way around at this stage and make sure your pattern aligns on the straight grain.

04 Next, give your fabric a really good iron to remove all creases. Be sure also to get rid of any loose fibres. Place your fabric pattern-side down on to your work surface. I use masking tape to hold the fabric in position. Lay the PVC on top of the fabric and use some tailor's chalk or a soft pencil to mark around the edge of the PVC on to the fabric as a positional guide. If your fabric is patterned, pay close attention to getting it straight.

0 5 Peel back around 4in (10cm) of the PVC release paper. I tend to work from right to left. Position this 4in (10cm) section adhesive-side down on to your fabric, making sure to align everything with your chalk or pencil marks. Once in position, smooth and stick down this first section. Remove the rest of the PVC release paper bit by bit, using the same positioning, smoothing and sticking action. I pull the release paper with my left hand and smooth with my right. Check you have no air bubbles or creases as you smooth and stick. Working from the middle out helps.

0 6 Next, cut back any excess fabric to leave an allowance of ¾in (2cm) borders along the long top and bottom edges, and ⅜in (1cm) on one of the short ends. The other end should be trimmed in line with the edge of the PVC. I use small embroidery scissors to do this, so that I can get in really tight to the edge.

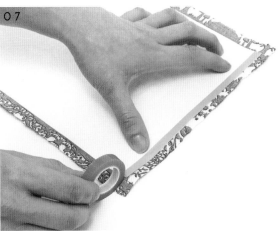

0 7 Taking the short end with the ⅜in (1cm) border, run a piece of double-sided tape along the width of the PVC.

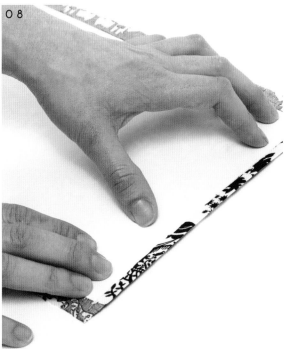

0 8 Remove the tape backing then fold the ⅜in (1cm) fabric border over it, so that you get a really crisp finishing edge.

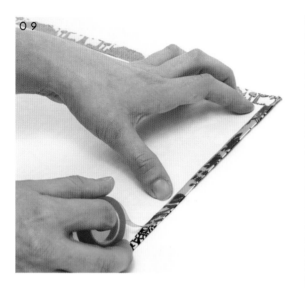

09 Stick another length of double-sided tape on top of the fabric you have just folded over, making sure that it is as close to the edge as possible. This will be used to stick the seam. Do not remove the backing tape yet.

10 Taking the rings, run double-sided tape along each of them. Try to keep the tape centred. If the fabric has a directional pattern, make sure that the frame is the right way up for your end use. For example, with the gimbal ring at the bottom the frame can be used on a table lamp, while with the gimbal ring at the top it will work only as a pendant shade. A way to be more flexible is to use a plain fabric or one that has a pattern that works in any orientation. Always make sure that the gimbal faces in, and not out, regardless of usage. Here, I am making a table lamp.

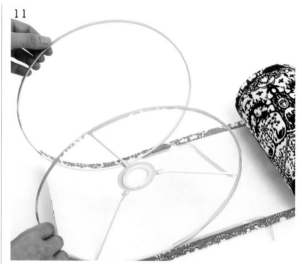

11 Now you are ready to add the fabric to the frame. Start at the opposite end of the fabric to where you put the seam tape. Remove the backing from the end of the double-sided tape on the rings, and position on the edges of the PVC panel. Working carefully, and using both hands, remove the tape bit by bit on each ring as you roll the frame along the edges of the panel. Make sure you keep the ring wires in line with the edges of the panel of PVC. Stop about 1½in (4cm) from the end.

12 Remove the backing from the seam tape and finish rolling the rings along the edges of the PVC until the two ends of the fabric overlap one another. Now press down firmly on both panels from the inside of the shade, to create a clean, crisp seam.

13 Make a small incision with your scissors where each of the three gimbal struts meet the ring.

14 With either the flat edge of the rolled-edge serrated tool or an old store card, work carefully around each ring pushing the excess border fabric so that it is tucked away behind the ring. Do this top and bottom. You need to apply quite a lot of pressure. Long fingernails also help!

15

15 You now have your finished shade!

EMBELLISHING YOUR SHADE

You can add embellishments if you like. Pompoms always look great, as does ric rac. This can be attached using the double-sided tape or some fabric glue. Make sure you have the lampshade the right way up when you add trims, and have it at eye level when you attach them. This can be done easily by putting the lampshade on a lamp base.

💡 GET INSPIRED

For a whole array of stunning drum lampshades, have a look at the creations by Miranda Law of Swee Mei Lampshades (*see page 178*).

FRAME TYPE: No frame required

TECHNIQUE: Fabric remnants with self-adhesive lampshade PVC, to create 10 mini-shades for fairy lights

PROJECT TIME: 2 hours

SKILL LEVEL: 🔦 🔦 🔦 🔦 🔦

FAIRY LANTERNS

A GARLAND OF PRETTY LIGHTS WITH WHICH TO FESTOON YOUR HOME

FABRIC & DECORATION:

 5 pieces of fabric, approximately 8½in (21cm) x 11¾in (30cm). This is an ideal project for using up remnants. For this example, I used off-cuts from four vintage scarves.

TIP

Your fairy lights do not have to be the exact length suggested here. It very much depends on the length of lights you can get hold of. You can also mix and match the shape of the lanterns. (See page 57 for some ideas.)

TOOLS & MATERIALS

- 10 paper fasteners, white
- piece of polystyrene
- glue
- 10 buttons
- self-adhesive lampshade PVC
- paper scissors
- steam iron
- fabric scissors
- leather hole punch
- set of 10 LED fairy lights

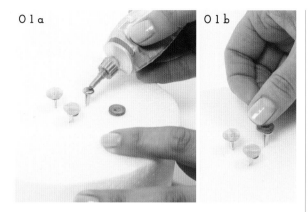

01 You need to attach your buttons to the paper fasteners in advance of constructing the mini shades, to allow time for the glue to fix. Begin by pushing the ten paper fasteners into the polystyrene – this holds them steady while you apply the glue. Add glue to the head of each fastener (a), then place a button on top and press down firmly to secure (b). Repeat this until all ten fasteners have buttons.

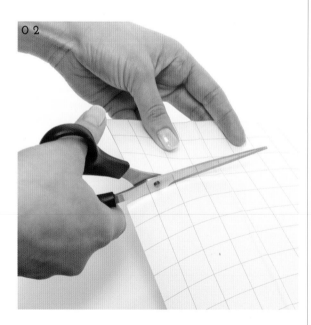

02 Cut the self-adhesive lampshade PVC into ten strips, each measuring 8 x 2³⁄₈in (20 x 6cm). Use paper scissors to do this. Put aside.

03 Iron your fabrics. It's very important to have beautiful, super-ironed fabric, as any creases will be seen and may spoil the finished look. Next, lay your fabrics on the table and take a few minutes moving the cut-out strips around the fabrics to work out which part of the print you want to use. If necessary, cut your fabrics to a workable size.

04 Make sure your workspace is clean and free from loose threads. You are now ready to get sticking. Turn the fabric over so that the wrong side is face up. Take one of the PVC strips and peel back about 1¹⁄₂in (4cm) of the backing paper and place on the fabric. Continue to peel back with one hand, while carefully pressing down the PVC with the other hand.

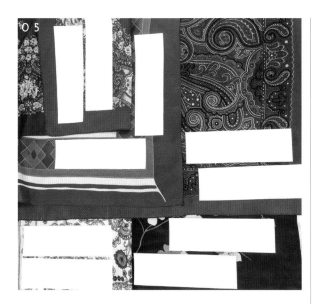

0 5 Continue to stick down each strip on your selected sections of fabric.

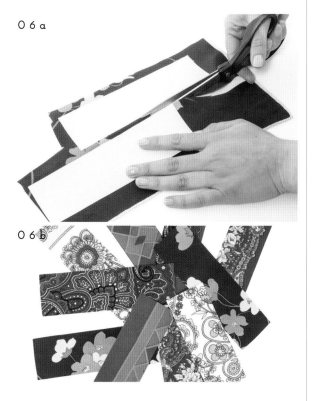

0 6 Once all ten strips are stuck down, you can carefully cut the excess fabric from around the PVC with sharp fabric scissors (a, b).

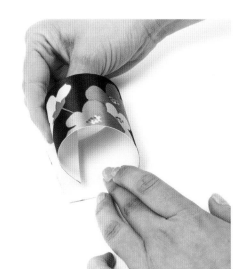

0 7 Roll each strip of fabric and its PVC backing into a tube, so that the ends are overlapping by about ³/4in (2cm).

0 8 Using a leather hole punch on setting 3.5, punch a hole near the centre of the overlap as close to the edge as possible.

09a

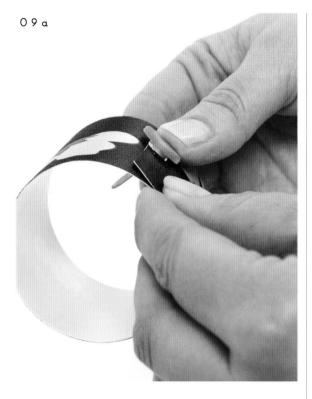

10

10 Now, punch a larger hole in each shade for the LED light to fit through. Using the larger setting of 4.5, make a hole above or below the button, and about 3/8in (1cm) away from the overlapping edge.

09b

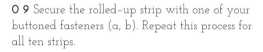

09 Secure the rolled-up strip with one of your buttoned fasteners (a, b). Repeat this process for all ten strips.

11

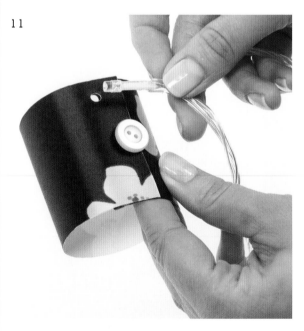

11 Take a set of LED fairy lights and unwind. Using a little force, push each individual light through the hole in each shade. Be sure to push through only the light, and not the wire.

12 Once all the mini shades are attached to their lights, you're ready to add the batteries. Then, your beautiful fairy lanterns are complete. Enjoy.

TIPS

• Instead of buttons, you can paint the tops of the fasteners in different colours or cover them in lightweight paper. You could also use a button-making kit and cover the buttons in the same or a contrasting fabric.

• If you find the hole is not big enough, take your scissors and cut lengthways and horizontally across the hole in an X shape and try again. The lights should fit through this time.

• You do not have to restrict yourself to this shape of lantern; you could finish the edges off with scallop shapes or you could create funnel-shaped shades instead.

💡 GET INSPIRED

Sally Whiting of Made by Sally Whiting contributed to this step-by-step tutorial. Take a look at her fabulous lampshades on page 170.

FRAME TYPE: Coolie top and bottom ring with duplex fitting

TECHNIQUE: Rolled fabric and self-adhesive lampshade PVC

PROJECT TIME: 2.5 hours

SKILL LEVEL: ♀ ♀ ♀ ♀ ♀

DOTTY LOVE

DITSY POLKA DOTS COUPLED WITH BIG, BOLD BLOOMS

FABRIC & DECORATION:

Big Blooms by Kaffe Fassett,
40in (1m) square

TOOLS & MATERIALS

- tape measure
- brown paper, 40in (1m) square
- marker pen
- ruler
- set square
- string, 40in (1m)
- pencil
- self-adhesive lampshade PVC
- paper scissors
- steam iron
- fabric scissors
- double-sided tape
- rolled-edge serrated tool,
  or an old store card

TIP

Your top and bottom rings may be a fixed size,
but you can make your coolie any height you wish.
You could go for a 1960s retro look and create an
oversized funnel with a bold, solid base to sit on
the floor. Try out this simple coolie first and then
try experimenting with shade height.

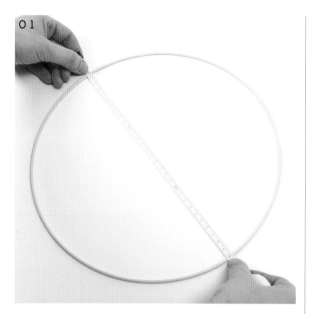

01 In order to make a template from brown paper you need to start by measuring the diameter of the frame's bottom ring.

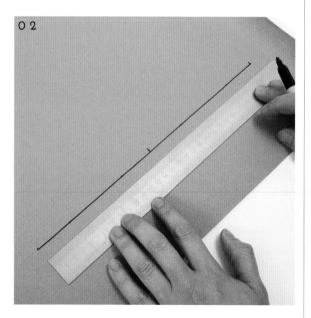

02 In the bottom right-hand corner of the brown paper, use a pen and ruler to draw a line equal to the diameter measurement. In this case it is 12in (30cm). This line is Line A. Mark the centrepoint at 6in (15cm).

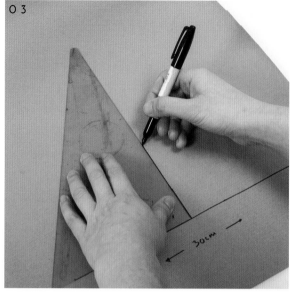

03 Use a set square to mark a perpendicular line from the centrepoint. This is Line B.

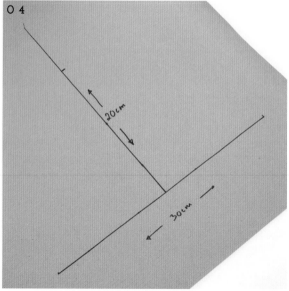

04 Extend Line B to the height of your shade. It's up to you how tall you wish to make it. Here, I have chosen 8in (20cm).

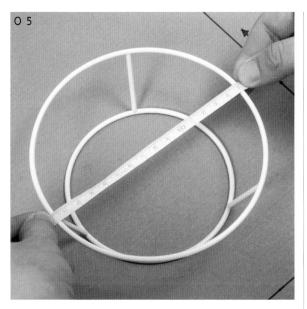

0 5 Measure the diameter of the top ring. Here it is 6in (15cm).

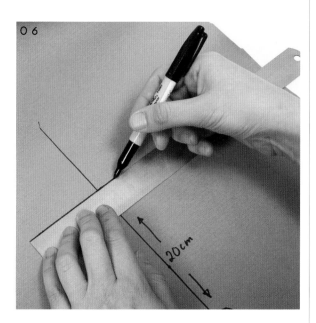

0 6 Draw a horizontal line at the top of Line B, equal to the diameter of the top ring. Make sure that it is centred. This is Line C.

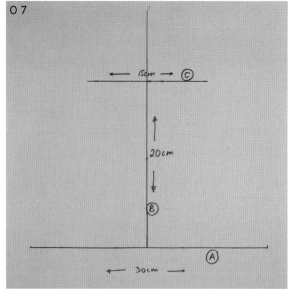

0 7 You now have the key dimensions of your lampshade marked on the paper.

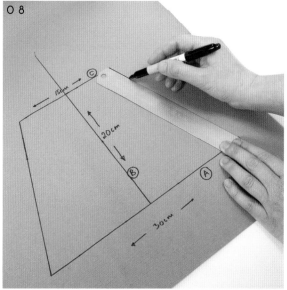

0 8 Join the ends of Line A and Line C to create a trapezoid shape.

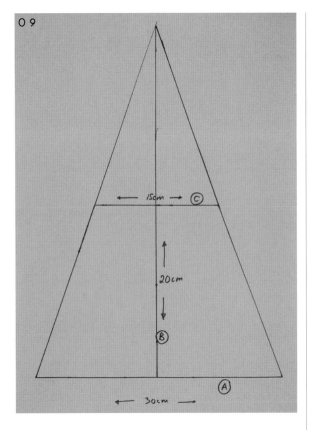

09 Extend the lines you have just drawn up until they meet at the point of a triangle. Extend Line B up to meet them. The point where all three lines converge will be your pivot point.

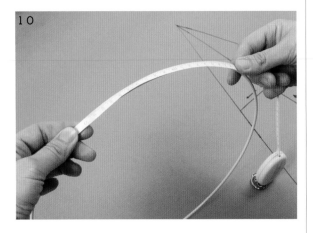

10 With the tape measure, measure the circumference of the bottom ring. You will need to measure this for step 13.

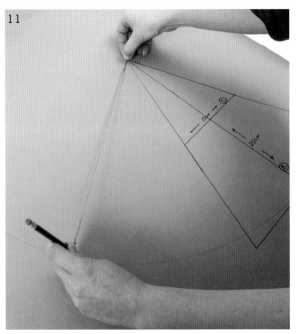

11 Tie the string around a pencil. Position the point of the pencil at the centrepoint on Line A. Then, keeping the string taut stretch it up to the pivot point. Holding the string firmly on the pivot point, draw a curved line from the centrepoint on Line A all the way up to the top of your piece of paper. Then, swing the pencil back past the centrepoint on Line A, and continue your curved line until it hits the right-hand angle of your triangle.

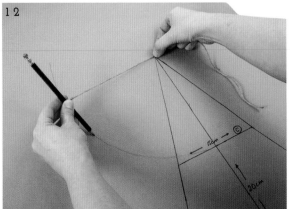

12 Create a second curved line by following the same process, but this time starting with the point of the pencil positioned at the centrepoint on Line C.

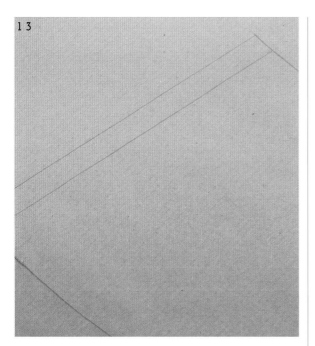

13 To check your template, cut a piece of string equal to the circumference of the bottom ring, here 37in (94cm). Run the string along the first of your curved lines and mark 37in (94cm). Do the same with the second curved line by measuring the circumference of the top ring and using this as your length. Join both curved lines together with a straight line, and add around ³/₄in (2cm) for the overlap.

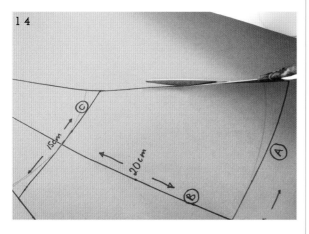

14 Carefully cut out your template.

15 Lay your template on the backing paper of the self-adhesive lampshade PVC and draw around it. Cut out the marked piece of PVC.

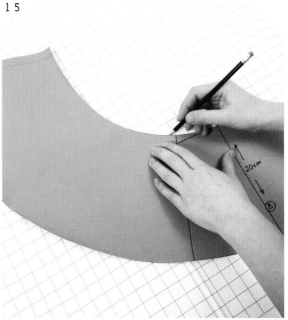

16 Iron your fabric, and place it face down on the work surface. Position the PVC to get the best of the fabric pattern, and carefully release the backing paper to stick it in position. Turn over and smooth out any creases or air bubbles.

17 Allow for a ⅜in (1cm) seam at one end, and ⅝in (1.5cm) along the curved edges top and bottom. Draw pencil lines to mark these measurements.

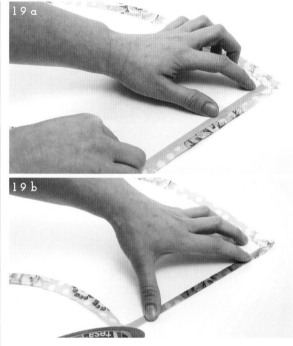

19 Run some double-sided tape along the edge of the other end (a). Remove the backing, and fold the fabric seam allowance over to stick and create a crisp edge (b). Run another length of tape along the folded fabric seam, but do not release the backing tape yet.

18 Cut the fabric along your pencil lines. When you come to the end without the seam allowance, cut flush to the PVC.

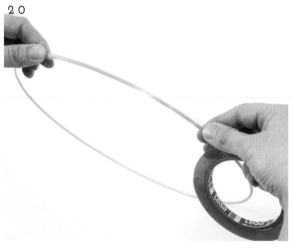

20 Run double-sided tape along the edges of the bottom and top rings.

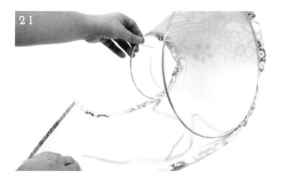

2 1 Carefully and slowly release a small amount of backing tape from both rings, and start to run them along the edges of the PVC as shown. This can be fiddly, but persevere.

2 2 When you have almost reached the end, release the backing tape from the overlap and firmly press the ends together. This will hold the lampshade fast.

2 3 Make a small incision with scissors at the point where the gimbal meets the top ring. In this case there were three points.

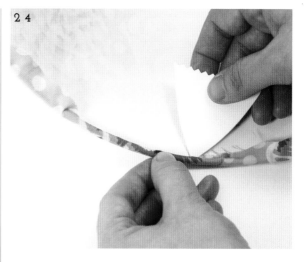

2 4 Using the rolled-edge serrated tool or an old store card, push the excess fabric under the top and bottom rings, effectively tucking it in.

2 5

2 5 The finished shade sits very pretty.

FRAME TYPE: Drum top and bottom ring with pendant gimbal fitting

TECHNIQUE: Self-adhesive lampshade PVC to create a double-sided drum lampshade for a ceiling pendant

PROJECT TIME: 2.5 hours

SKILL LEVEL: 🔆🔆🔆🔆🔆

DISCO DIGITALE

SURE TO GET YOU IN THE MOOD FOR DANCING

FABRIC & DECORATION

Hapi by Amy Butler, for the outer fabric, 40in (1m) wide x 12in (30cm) drop

Chevron pattern by Timeless Treasures, for the lining, 40in (1m) wide x 12in (30cm) drop

TOOLS & MATERIALS

- tape measure
- self-adhesive lampshade PVC
- paper scissors
- steam iron
- flame retardant spray
- masking tape
- small embroidery scissors
- pencil
- long ruler
- double-sided tape
- pegs
- rolled-edge serrated tool, or old store card

TIP

An alternative to using two patterned fabrics is to use a pale, solid-coloured linen on the outside and a bold patterned fabric on the lining. This way you will have a fairly conservative-looking lampshade when it's not illuminated and a bold and arresting lampshade when it's switched on. It's a great way of transforming a living space in the evening.

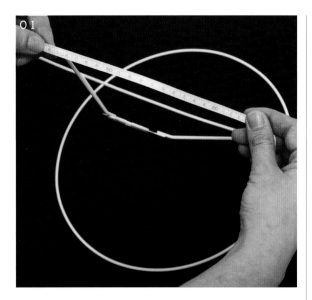

0 1 Measure the circumference of your top and bottom rings. This will determine the width of your shade. The height is up to you. In this case I have used a 37½in (95cm) circumference with an 8¾in (22cm) height. Make sure you add ¾in (2cm) to the circumference measurement for the overlap.

0 3 Select your lining fabric. Here I am using a bold chevron design. Iron your fabric very carefully to get rid of any creases. Then you need to treat the fabric with flame retardant spray, following the guidelines (*see page 27*). Once the fabric is completely dry, lay it pattern side down on your work surface. Secure the fabric in place with masking tape. Now, take your cut piece of PVC and place it on top of the lining fabric. Take your time to position the PVC correctly. If your fabric has a distinct pattern, be sure to line things up. In this case, I used the vertical lines of my chosen fabric as a point of reference. Draw around your piece of PVC.

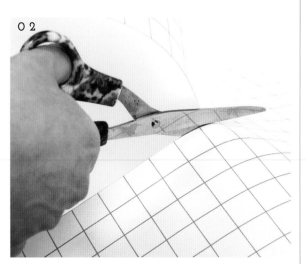

0 2 Measure out the self-adhesive lampshade PVC using the above dimensions and use paper scissors to cut to size. You can use the grid as a cutting guide to make sure you get straight lines.

0 4 Once you are happy with the position, peel a little of the backing paper off one side of the PVC and stick it in place on the fabric. Remember all the time to keep the fabric as flat as possible and coax out any bubbles or creases. Work your way along the fabric until the whole length of PVC is stuck. Turn it over and make sure there are no creases.

0 5 Trim the fabric with fabric scissors. You need to cut as close to the edge of the PVC as possible all the way around. I use small embroidery scissors for this purpose as you can get in really tight to the PVC.

0 7 Slowly peel some of the backing paper away from the PVC and begin carefully sticking it down on the fabric as before. Smooth as you go and make sure you keep an eye on the position and your pencil guidelines.

0 8 Once all the PVC is firmly stuck down, check both sides of the PVC to make sure there are no creases or air bubbles.

0 6 Select your outer fabric and iron it. Place it pattern side down on your work surface. Use masking tape to secure. Place your piece of PVC on top, with the pattern of the lining fabric facing up. Position the PVC carefully to make the best of the pattern on your outer fabric. With a pencil and long ruler draw around the PVC, allowing for a $5/8$in (1.5cm) seam along the top and bottom and a $3/8$in (1cm) seam at one of the ends. The other end will be trimmed right up to the PVC, so needs no seam allowance.

0 9 When you are happy with the finish, cut around your $5/8$in (1.5cm) pencil guidelines along the top and bottom using fabric scissors. Then, cut along the $3/8$in (1cm) pencil guideline at one end. At the other end, trim the fabric so that it is flush with the PVC.

10 Along the edge of the end with the ³⁄₈in (1cm) seam allowance, place a line of double-sided tape as close to the PVC edge as possible.

11 Peel off the backing from the tape, and fold the ³⁄₈in (1cm) of fabric over to create a crisp edge. Now, put another strip of double-sided tape on top of this, but do not remove the backing.

12 Run a line of double-sided tape along each ring of the frame. Make sure the gimbal always faces inwards. In this case I am making a pendant lampshade, so I need to make sure the gimbal ring is at the top of my shade. If you were making a table lamp, it would need to be at the bottom. This is only relevant when the fabric you are using has an obvious directional pattern.

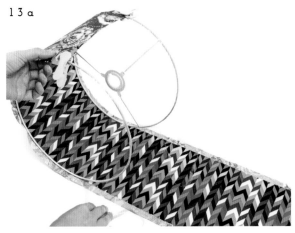

13 a

13 b

13 Peel a small section of backing tape off both lampshade rings and position on the PVC so that the lining fabric is facing up (a). Remember to check whether you are making a pendant or table lamp and keep the gimbal facing inwards at all times. Try to keep each ring as close to the edge of the laminate as possible. You may need to use a couple of pegs to secure it in place while you roll the rings along the whole length of the PVC, carefully removing the backing from the tape as you go (b). This bit can be quite fiddly so if you have a spare pair of hands to call on, do, it will help enormously.

14 When you are nearly at the end of the PVC, remove the strip of backing tape from the overlap and press the join firmly into place.

15 Make a small incision in the fabric at the three points where the gimbal fitting meets the ring.

16 Using the rolled-edge serrated tool, start to work the excess fabric under the ring using a tucking action. You will hear some cracking sounds, but don't be alarmed as this is perfectly normal.

17 Once all the fabric is tucked under both top and bottom rings you are finished. You can go on to add trim if you wish. I haven't here as I feel the shade is busy enough, but if you have used a less vibrant combination of fabrics then some trim might work well. It's a matter of personal taste, so experiment and see what works best for you.

💡 GET INSPIRED

Designer-makers creating truly beautiful double-sided drums include Lampara (*see page 168*) and Timorous Beasties (*see page 180*).

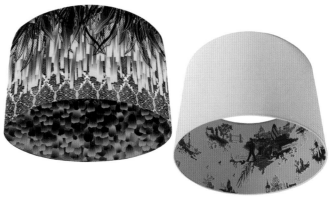

FRAME TYPE: Rectangular pagoda

TECHNIQUE: Multi-panelled hard-sided lampshade using self-adhesive lampshade PVC and double-sided tape

PROJECT TIME: 3.5 hours

SKILL LEVEL: 💡💡💡💡💡

MAUDE DECO

AN EXOTIC FEAST OF COLOURS AND PATTERN CONJURING UP FAR-OFF LANDS

FABRIC & DECORATION

 vintage silk scarf, approx. 40in (1m) square

 aqua gimp, 2¼yd (2m)

 peacock blue bullion fringing, 60in (1.5m)

TOOLS & MATERIALS

- plump cushion
- brown paper
- marker pen
- paper scissors
- small coloured stickers
- self-adhesive lampshade PVC
- steam iron
- small embroidery scissors
- double-sided tape
- fabric tape
- glue
- wooden stirrer
- pegs

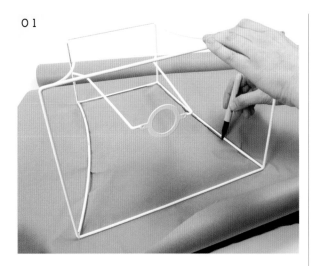

01 This frame does not need to be bound. Create a template for each panel using a plump cushion and some brown paper. To achieve a true impression of the panel, push the frame gently into the cushion. Run a marker pen around the inside of the panel.

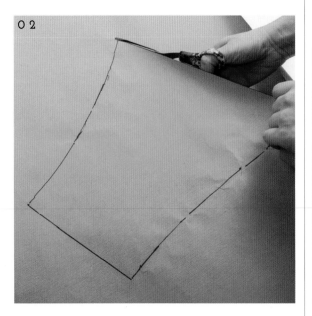

02 Cut the panel out, and repeat for each panel. It's a good idea to number or colour code each frame panel and paper template to ensure you match the correct template to its corresponding panel. I use small coloured stickers. I always put the sticker on the side of the paper template that will face out of the lampshade.

03 Lay out your self-adhesive lampshade PVC with the grid side up, and position your paper templates with their identifying stickers facing up. Trace around each template with a pencil. Remember to colour code each PVC panel to match the paper templates. This time, however, put the sticker on the laminate, not on the backing paper.

04 Cut out the PVC panels. Lay each panel on top of your fabric to get a rough idea of the area of pattern you would like to use for each panel.

O 5

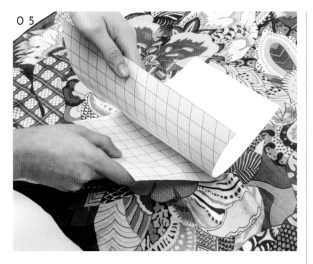

O 5 Iron your fabric well to remove all creases, then lay flat on a large work surface right side down. When you are certain of the position, remove the backing paper from each PVC panel and stick down on to the fabric. Smooth out each panel to get rid of any air bubbles or creases.

O 6

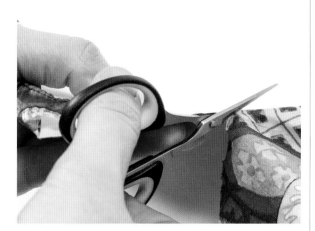

O 6 Using some small embroidery scissors, cut around each PVC panel tight to the edge to remove excess fabric.

O 7

O 7 Here you can see a finished panel.

O 8

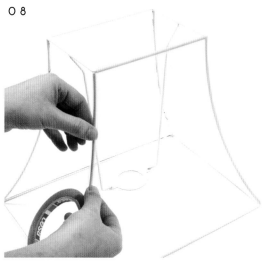

O 8 Taking the frame, run double-sided tape up the struts and along the top and bottom of one panel.

09

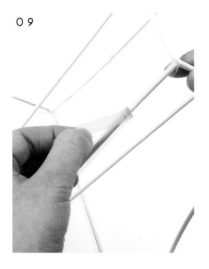

09 Remove all the backing from the tape.

10 a

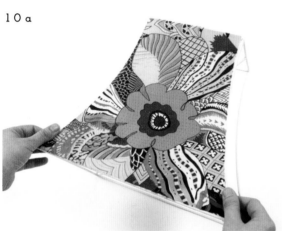

10 b

10 Make sure you have the correct PVC panel for the matching frame panel. Carefully position the PVC panel over the frame panel, with the fabric facing out (a). Now press firmly against the struts, and the top and bottom rings, to stick the panel in place (b). Follow steps 8, 9 and 10 for each panel.

11

11 If you have PVC sticking out on any strut, you can trim this back with scissors. Run a length of fabric tape along each strut where the panels meet, just to help secure them in place. Before you do so, make sure your trim is wide enough to cover the fabric tape.

12

12 Working down from the top ring, use glue to stick your trim to each strut. The trim should cover up the fabric tape.

13 When each strut is finished, apply trim to the top ring using the same method. I use plastic pegs to hold the trim in place while the glue dries.

14 Finally, add the fringing to the bottom ring. Again, I use pegs to hold the fringe in place as I work around the frame.

15 When all the glue is dry, remove the pegs and, 'Hey, Deco!' You will have a beautiful lampshade.

> **TIP**
> You could totally mix this project up and use sections of different vintage silk scarves for each panel. If you have double-sided laminated PVC you could also line the inside of the shade in a complementary fabric. There are so many options available. If you decide to apply this technique to a suspended lampshade then making a feature of the lining makes sense as it will more often than not been seen from below. Being a fan of bold fabrics and pattern clashing I would even recommend using a different fabric for each panel of the lining.

FRAME TYPE: Hexagonal candle x 3

TECHNIQUE: Two-panelled, soft-sided lampshades using machine stitching and hand sewing

PROJECT TIME: 6 hours (2 hours per shade)

SKILL LEVEL: ♀ ♀ ♀ ♀ ♀

BOTANICA

THE THREE GRACES IN BOLD FLORALS

FABRIC & DECORATION

 various hand-drawn *Garden* patterns by Anna Maria Horner, 3 Fat Quarters (FQs)

 lime and red VV Rouleaux tassel fringing, 12in (30cm)

orange and pink VV Rouleaux tassel fringing, 12in (30cm)

 yellow beaded fringing, 12in (30cm)

 ³⁄₈in (10mm) orange ribbon, 20in (50cm)

³⁄₈in (1cm) deep-pink velvet ribbon, 12in (30cm)

TOOLS & MATERIALS

- binding tape
- steam iron
- lills
- tailor's chalk
- pencil
- dressmaking pins
- sewing machine
- overlocker (optional)
- fabric scissors
- bold thread
- thimble
- glue
- pegs
- wooden stirrer

O 1

O 1 The frame has already been covered in binding. I have chosen black binding on this occasion. (For instructions on how to bind the frame, see page 32.) The three frames used here have permanent binding on the top and bottom rings, and temporary binding on two opposite struts.

O 2

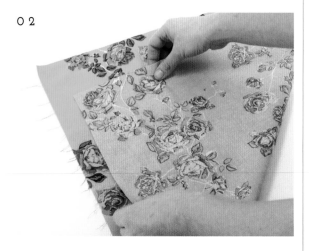

O 2 Iron your fabric well. Take one FQ and fold in half, right side to right side so you are working on the bias. You will need one FQ for each of the three candle shades. Make sure the fabric's wrong side faces out.

O 3

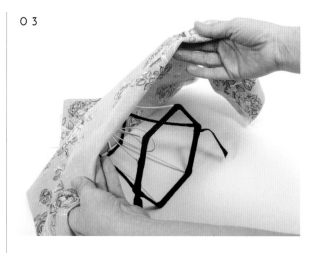

O 3 Take what is now a triangle of two layers of fabric, and drape over one side of your frame. It should stretch easily from one of the bound side struts to the other.

O 4

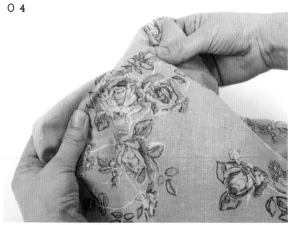

O 4 Make sure that you have at least 2in (5cm) excess fabric top and bottom, and on both sides.

0 5

0 5 Once you are happy with the position of the fabric, start pinning. Using lills, pin out the fabric at the four corners where the bound struts meet the top and bottom rings. Make sure the pins go through both layers of fabric and the binding cotton, and always pin away from the frame.

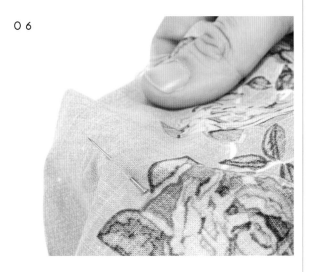

0 6

0 6 Stretching the fabric, carefully add lills to the centre of each top and bottom ring, and then to each strut. You need to mirror each lill with another lill, to make sure you are not pulling the fabric excessively in one direction.

0 7

0 7 Continue to add lills in this way, stretching the fabric as you go, until the sandwiched fabric is completely pinned to the frame. You should have lills at intervals of approximately ⅜in (1cm).

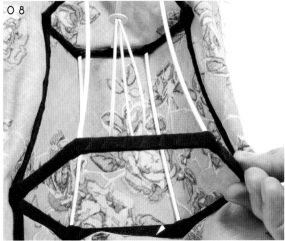

0 8

0 8 Go around the whole frame again, stretching and repinning the fabric to ensure a really snug fit. Check inside the frame regularly to make sure both layers of fabric are taut and not just the outer layer — otherwise your final fit will be off.

09 You can test whether your fabric is stretched sufficiently by tapping it with the back of your hand. If it sounds like a drum, it's taut enough. Using tailor's chalk or a soft pencil, draw lines on your fabric along each strut. Make sure the line follows the line of the strut exactly. Extend the lines top and bottom by at least 1½in (4cm).

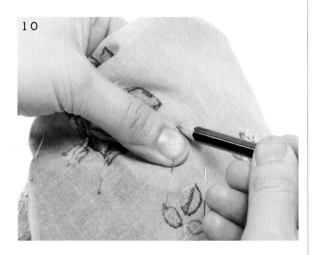

10 Now run your hand carefully along the top ring. Every time you reach a strut, measure out a thumb's length and insert the point of a pencil through both layers of fabric to create a hole.

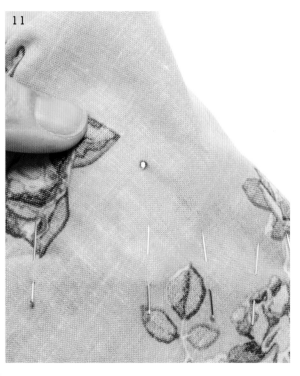

11 The holes will act as extra guides in where to position the cover when you come to put it back on the frame. Make pencil holes at each strut along the top and bottom rings.

12 Secure your fabric by pinning both layers together around the edge with dressmaking pins. Make sure that the fabrics are flat and there are no creases or puckered areas. Check both sides as you pin. You can always tack stitch, if you prefer.

1 3

1 3 You are now ready to carefully remove all the lills, but not the dressmaking pins. The result should look like this.

1 4

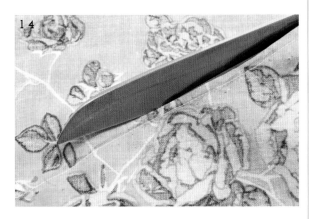

1 4 Machine stitch down each pencil line. I tend to use a straight stitch, but you can use a zigzag stitch to allow for more give. This is particularly useful if the fabric you are using isn't super stretchy. You can overlock the seams, too, to make them more durable. Trim the excess fabric off from your cover, leaving about a ¼in (5mm) seam allowance. Make sure you are cutting into the selvedge, not your lampshade!

1 5

1 5 Do not cut any fabric off the top and bottom, only the sides. At this stage, your cover should look like this.

1 6

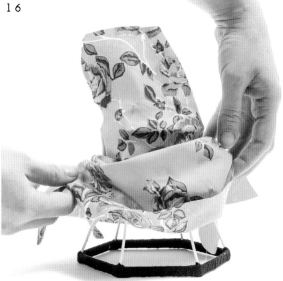

1 6 Take the temporary binding off each strut. Turn your lampshade cover right side out. Slip it over the frame in much the same way you would put on a dress over your head.

17 Line up each seam with the two opposing side struts opposing. Pin to the top and bottom ring, using lills and working away from the frame.

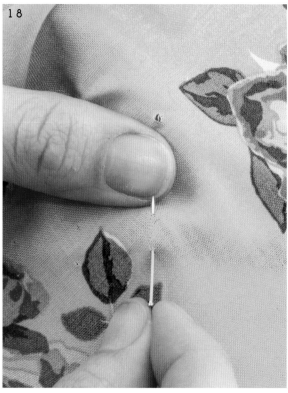

18 Line up each pencil hole with the remaining struts at the point where they meet the top and bottom rings. Pin here, using lills.

STRAIGHT VERSUS BIAS

You can sometimes use the straight of the fabric to cover the frame, but this will depend on the shape of the frame and the stretchiness of the fabric you are using. I always err on the side of caution, and go with the bias.

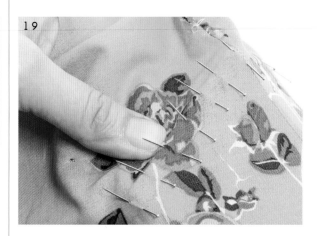

19 The lills should be about ³⁄₈in (1cm) apart.

2 0

2 1 Once the fabric is pinned out, stitch the cover to the frame using bold thread and the streetly stitch (*see page 36*). Remember to keep stretching the fabric as you stitch. This is why you shouldn't trim back the excess fabric top and bottom until you have stitched, as you can use the excess fabric to help pull the shade taut. Be sure to keep the stitching on the outer edge of each ring, as you want to be able to hide the stitching with the trim. Remove the lills as you stitch. Remember to use a thimble when stitching, or your fingers will get very sore.

2 0 Stretch and manipulate the fabric as you pin, to make sure it fits on the frame without any puckering. The fabric should be taut. As before, work your way around the shade stretching and repinning until it is perfect. It can take a lot longer than you think to pin the cover successfully, so stick at it. Tap with the back of your hand to test that it is taut enough.

> **TIP**
> Always make sure seams are aligned with the corresponding strut. Keep them as narrow as possible without jeopardizing the quality and strength of your shade. Cut seams as straight as possible and never iron flat, as they will show up when the lamp is turned on.

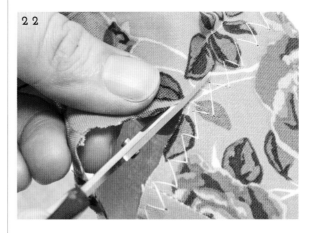

2 2 Once the stitching is finished, you can trim away the excess fabric from the top and bottom rings. If you are going to add lining, now is the time to do it (*see page 41*). In this instance I am not adding lining, as these frames are very small and the fabric I have used for the outer covers is a fairly heavy cotton.

2 3

2 3 You are now ready to add the trim. Make sure the lampshade is at eye level. Putting it on a lamp base will help enormously.

TIP
Paper glue can be used to fix stitches and the trimmed fabric edge. Put a bit on your finger and just massage it into the area you want.

2 4

2 4 Start with the top ring. Carefully apply glue to a small section of the trim, and stick to the side of the top ring to cover the stitching. Use pegs to hold the trim in place while you work your way around the shade and the glue dries. To finish off, create a ⅜in (1cm) overlap with the trim.

2 5

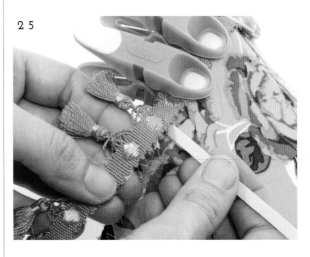

2 5 Finally, attach the trim to the bottom ring in the same way, always making sure to cover up the stitching so it looks professional.

26

2 6 One finished shade.

💡 **GET INSPIRED**
Designer-makers creating truly beautiful soft-sided shades in this manner include Rockville (*see page 174*) and Zoë Darlington (*see page 182*). Have a look at their work, then let your imagination run wild.

2 7 Repeat the whole process, to create three graceful shades like these.

2 7

FRAME TYPE: Bowed Empire

TECHNIQUE: Multi-panelled soft-sided lampshade using glue

PROJECT TIME: 3.5 hours

SKILL LEVEL: 🔦🔦🔦🔦🔦

FRIDA ROCKS

A STRIPY, FLORAL RIOT OF TEAL, LIME, PINK, RED AND BROWN

FABRIC & DECORATION

Ooh la la by Pillow & Maxfield for Michael Miller, 20in (50cm)

Candy Stripes by Timeless Fabrics, 20in (50cm)

Ta Dot by Michael Miller in lime and teal, 40in (1m)

lime and red V V Rouleaux tassel fringing, 118in (3m)

lime polka dot bias binding, 40in (1m)

³⁄₈in (1cm) antique pink grosgrain ribbon, 118in (3m)

brown ric rac, 118in (3m)

teal ric rac, 40in (1m)

TOOLS & MATERIALS

- plump cushion
- brown paper
- marker pen
- paper scissors
- dressmaking pins
- tailor's chalk or soft pencil
- fabric scissors or pinking shears
- sewing machine
- embroidery scissors
- pegs
- fabric glue
- wooden stirrer

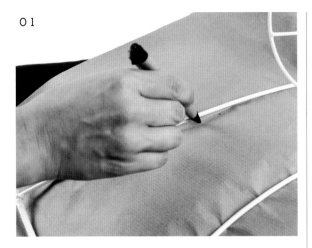

01 First you need to create a panel template. To do this, find a plump cushion, place brown paper on top of it, then turn your frame on its side and gently push into the paper to get a true impression of one of the panels. Draw around the inside of the panel frame to create the shape of its template. Make sure that you maintain pressure on the frame, to attain an accurate shape and ensure there is as little distortion as possible.

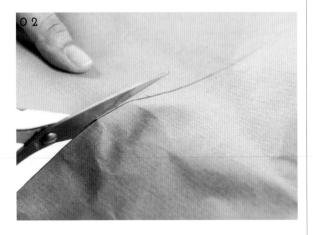

02 In this instance, I only need to create one template as all the panels are the same shape and size. However, you will work with frames that have different-sized panels, in which case you will need to create as many templates as there are panel shapes. Carefully cut out your template using paper scissors.

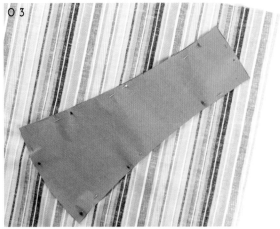

03 Make sure your fabric is on the bias (*see box below*). It is very important that the fabric is right side down, and that you pin out your template to the wrong side of the fabric.

04 Once you have pinned the template securely, draw around it with tailor's chalk. Use a colour that will show up clearly on the fabric you are using. You may have to use a soft pencil instead.

BIAS AND STRAIGHT GRAIN

Fabric is woven from two threads — the warp and the weft — that cross each other at right angles. When the fabric is cut along the line of either of these threads, it is being cut on the 'straight grain'. When fabric is cut diagonally across the threads, then it is being cut 'on the bias'. Bias-cut fabric is stretchier, drapes more and frays less than straight-cut fabric. To check you are on the bias, lay the fabric flat and use your hands to stretch the fabric apart. If there is no give whatsoever, you are dealing with the straight grain. If there is a lot of give and elasticity, your are on the bias.

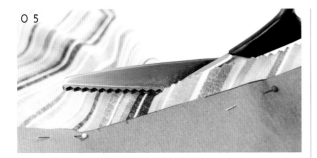

0 5 Cut out the fabric panel, allowing for a seam of at least 2in (5cm) along the top and bottom and ¾in (2cm) at the sides. You will need the extra fabric on the top and bottom so that you can stretch and manipulate the fabric over the frame. I use pinking shears to cut the fabric as the zigzag line helps reduce fraying. For this lampshade design you will need four panels of the stripy fabric shown here, and four panels of the floral fabric as it is an eight-panelled frame.

0 7 Pin the panels together in the order you want them to appear on the outside of the lampshade. I first pin two panels together (make sure the right sides of the fabrics are face to face, so that you stitch on the wrong side). Be as accurate as possible, matching the chalk lines on both panels. It may take a few attempts, but it will make all the difference to the finished shade.

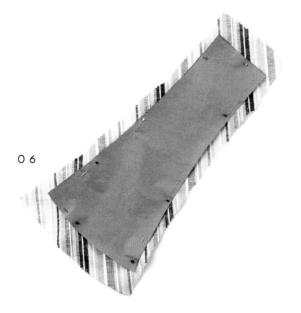

0 6 Repeat as many times as required, depending on the number of panels you need in any one fabric. Always check to make sure you are pinning on the bias. You need the stretch in the fabric to be widthways.

0 8 When you are happy with your pinning, sew the panels together using a sewing machine and running stitch. A very small stitch is advisable as there will be pull between the panels when they are attached to the frame, and you don't want to see the stitching or any gaps left by large stitching. Sew all the way to the end of the top of the panel and to the end of the bottom of the panel, as you don't want the stitched panel to be too short for the frame.

09

09 Once you have stitched together all the panels, you will have created what looks like a skirt. You are now ready to try it on the frame.

10

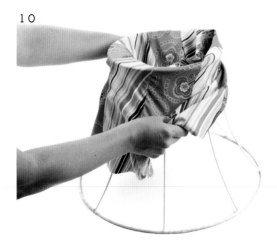

10 Before you trim any seams, make sure the 'skirt' fits over the frame. Once you are happy, trim all the seams down as small as possible using embroidery scissors. I usually try to leave a seam of as little as ¼in (5mm). You don't want bits of seam visible inside the lampshade when you shine light through it. Make sure that you also remove all the stray bits of thread or frayed fabric that might have attached itself to the panels. If you don't remove this you'll be able to see it when the light shines through the material.

11a

11 Fit the sewn panels to the frame with pegs (a, b). This is done to make sure the fabric stretches and fits in all the right places. I tend to start at the top ring and peg this out first, then I roll the frame on to its side with the top still pegged and start pegging out the bottom ring. You may have to work around the frame again adjusting pegs before you are happy with the tautness and position of the fabric. You need to align the seams with the struts. This is very important. And you want to avoid at all costs any puckering of the fabric because it hasn't been stretched sufficiently. The fabric needs to be stretched top and bottom, left to right and diagonally. It's all about manipulating the fabric to get it in the right place. This does take a bit of practice, but it's really worth persevering as it will affect the finish of your lampshade considerably.

11b

12

12 Once you are happy with how you've pegged out the fabric, you need to apply glue very carefully to the top ring. Be extremely careful not to drip any glue on the fabric, as this will ruin your cover straight away. You need to remove a couple of the pegs to work on one panel at a time. Stretch the fabric and peg to the top ring again, so that the glue can dry.

13

13 Glue the fabric to the bottom ring. Check all your pegs are still in the right place, the fabric is taut and there is no evidence of puckering. You can use a wooden stirrer to apply glue if you feel it gives you more control. As with the top ring, glue one panel at a time. Pull, push, stretch and tease the fabric into the exact place you want it. All seams should be lined up with the struts. It does take a lot of patience, but it really is worth it. Peg each panel back up again after gluing and leave to dry.

14

14 Now you can apply the trim to the shade. I start with the struts. Apply glue carefully to the centre of the trim and peg to the top of the frame in the correct position. Then glue and apply pressure to the trim all the way down the strut and panel seam until you get to the bottom of the frame. Peg here, too, and then begin the process on the next strut/seam. Do this all the way around the frame. Once the vertical trim is attached, you can add the trim to the top ring and the fringing to the bottom ring. Glue one panel at a time and make sure the fringing hangs in line with the base of the frame. Peg as you glue to hold the trim in place.

15

15 Your finished shade.

FRAME TYPE: Dome/half bowl

TECHNIQUE: Multi-panelled, soft-sided lampshade hand-stitched to the frame with integrated exterior lining and multicoloured binding tape

PROJECT TIME: 6 hours

SKILL LEVEL: ♀ ♀ ♀ ♀ ♀

LADY PENELOPE

A FELTED FANCY WITH BEADS, FAUX FLOWERS AND CROCHETED FLOWERS

FABRIC & DECORATION

bubblegum-pink felt, for the exterior lining, 40in (1m)

deep-blue felt, for the outer cover, 40in (1m)

heirloom crochet flowers, beads, faux flowers

red velvet ribbon, ¾in (2cm) wide, 3⅓yd (3m) long

red gimp, 12in (30cm)

multi-coloured pompom trim, approx. 60in (1.5m)

TOOLS & MATERIALS

- binding tape, multicoloured
- plump cushion
- brown paper
- marker pen
- dressmaking pins
- pencil
- fabric scissors
- sewing machine (optional)
- embroidery thread, various colours
- embroidery needle
- lills
- small embroidery scissors
- glue
- wooden stirrer
- pegs

O 1

O 1 This dome frame is bound in a multicoloured trim to create a feature. It will be suspended from the ceiling, so will be seen from underneath.

O 2

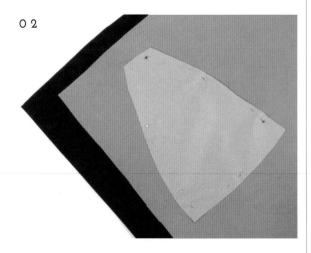

O 2 Create a paper template to suit your frame. This frame has 12 small panels, and I doubled up so that one template is wide enough for two panels. Using a cushion, follow Steps 1 and 2 on page 74. Lay the pink felt on top of the blue felt, and pin your template to the material.

O 3

O 3 Draw round your template, adding at least ³/4in (2cm) all the way around.

O 4

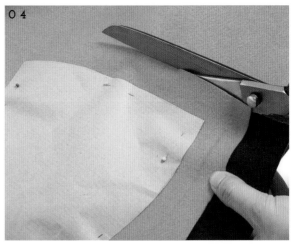

O 4 Cut along the line you have drawn, making sure you cut evenly through both pieces of felt.

O 5

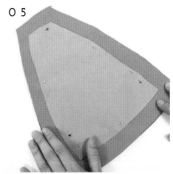

O 5 You now have one finished section. You will need to make another five to cover the 12 panels.

06

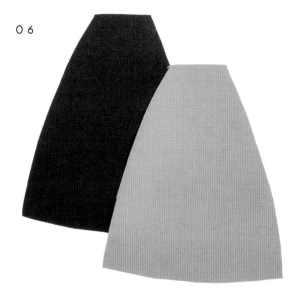

06 Make sure you make sections out of both the lining felt and the outer cover felt. Once all the sections are done, put the lining pieces to one side.

07

07 Decide how you wish to embellish your outer cover. I am using heirloom crochet flowers that belonged to my partner's grandma. As this lampshade is for our four-year old daughter's room, I wanted it to have a sense of family history. I have also put aside beads and faux flowers.

08a

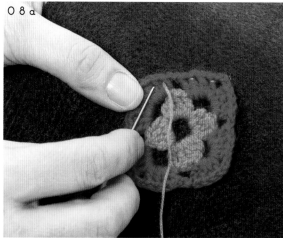

08b

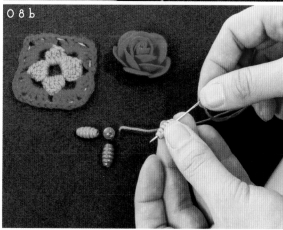

08 Machine or hand stitch your embellishments on to an outer felt section. I am hand stitching and using embroidery thread (a, b).

FANTASTIC FELT

Felt is an incredible material to work with. It is highly malleable and has an almost three-dimensional quality. It is also highly forgiving, which is a plus when it comes to lampshade making.

09 Repeat for each section. I varied each one, so that no two sections look quite the same.

10 When all the sections are ready, take one lining section (pink felt) and one outer section (blue felt), and sandwich them together with the embellishments facing out. This will hide all the stitching.

11 Now, drape the paired sections over the frame, so that the sandwiched sections work across two panels.

12 Start to pin the fabric out using lills.

13

13 Pin in each corner where the strut meets the top and bottom rings, and make sure the pins point away from the frame.

15

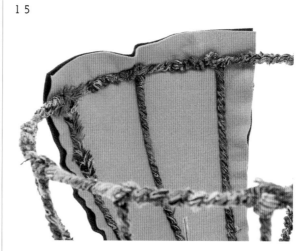

15 As you proceed, keep turning the frame over to check there are no creases or puckering in the lining.

14

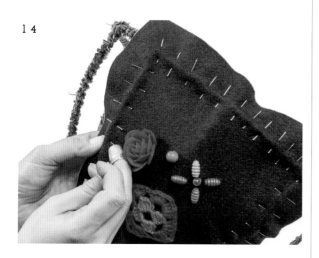

14 Keep adding pins, holding both pieces of fabric as taut as possible.

16

16 When you have pinned out the whole section, go back and work around the panels again, re-pinning and stretching the fabric as you go.

17 When you are happy with the tautness of your panels, begin stitching around the panel using the streetly stitch (*see page 36*), removing pins as you go. Be sure to keep hold of both pieces of fabric to keep things taut. Turn the frame over at regular intervals to check that the lining fabric is also taut.

18 When you have finished the first section, trim off excess fabric using small, sharp embroidery scissors. Cut close to your stitching, but avoid cutting any of your stitches or this will affect the stretch and finish of your shade. If you do cut into your stitches, overstitch immediately.

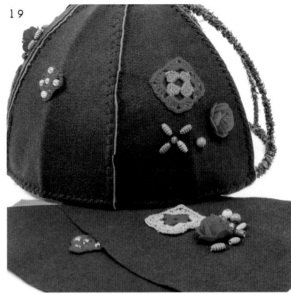

19 Continue with the other sections, until you have covered the whole frame. Remember to trim off the excess fabric each time you finish a section.

20 To attach the trim, start with the struts and work down from top ring to bottom ring. I am using velvet ribbon. Apply glue with a wooden stirrer and carefully attach the trim along the line of the strut or seam where two panels meet. Cover all stitching.

2 1 When all the struts have been trimmed, apply trim to the top ring in the same way. I am using gimp. You may need to use pegs to hold the trim in place. Finish with a ³⁄₈in (1cm) overlap. Again, be sure to cover up all the stitching.

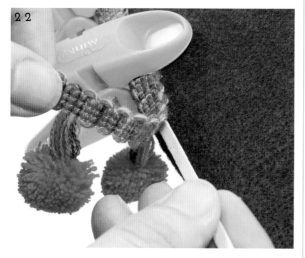

2 2 Finally, add the pompoms to the bottom ring. Try to do this at eye level. Even though this is a pendant shade, you can rest it on a table lamp base for this purpose. Apply glue with a wooden stirrer and work carefully around the bottom ring to attach the pompoms. Use pegs to hold the trim in place while the glue dries. Finish with a ³⁄₈in (1cm) overlap.

2 3 Lady Penelope has arrived.

💡 GET INSPIRED

Designer-makers creating truly beautiful lampshades using felt include Boris Design Studio (*see page 164*). Have a look at their work, then let your imagination run wild.

FRAME TYPE: Single-scalloped empire

TECHNIQUE: Multi-panelled, machine- and hand-stitched, soft-sided lampshade

PROJECT TIME: 4 hours

SKILL LEVEL: ○ ○ ○ ○ ○

BELLE TRIXIE

A BEAUTIFUL SPRINGTIME LAMPSHADE FOR THAT QUIET READING SPOT

FABRIC & DECORATION

 3 different Harlequin fabrics, 20in (50cm) square

 slate-grey gimp, 60in (1.5m)

 sage-green, large pompoms, 40in (1m)

TOOLS & MATERIALS

- cushion
- brown paper
- marker pen
- paper scissors
- iron
- dressmaking pins
- tailor's chalk
- fabric scissors
- sewing machine
- needle
- bold thread
- thimble
- wooden stirrer
- glue
- pegs

TIP
You can mix and match panel fabric as you desire.
You could make the shade in one single fabric design;
select two, and alternate panels; choose three like
I have done; or feature a different fabric on each
panel for a really unique look.

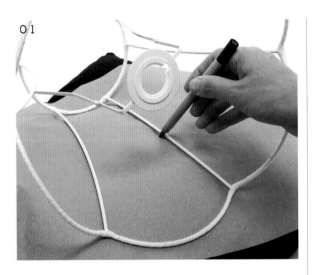

01

01 The frame is pre-bound, top and bottom rings. First, make the panel template. Plump up a cushion. Lay brown paper on the cushion, then put the frame on its side on top. With a marker pen, carefully draw around the inside of one of the panels – making sure you are pushing the frame down into the cushion to get a true impression of the surface area. Cut out your panel template.

02

02 Iron your fabric to remove creases. I have selected three different fabrics, so there will be two panels for each of the three fabrics (six in total). For each panel, you will need to lay the fabric right side down and make sure it is on the bias. Pin the paper template to the fabric. Draw around the template with tailor's chalk. Cut the template out, leaving a seam allowance of 5/8in (1.5cm) on each edge, and at least 2in (5cm) top and bottom. Remove the pins and repeat until you have all six panels cut out.

03

03 Next, you need to decide the order of your fabric panels on the lampshade. Once this is determined, you can machine stitch the panels together. To do this, lay two pieces of fabric together, with right sides facing and chalk lines aligned. Pin one edge along the chalk line. Then machine stitch along the edge, removing the pins as you go. Do the same with each panel until you have a 'skirt' of panels stitched together.

04

04 Trim off any excess fabric from your edge seams, leaving 3/8in (1cm) seam allowance. Next, fit the 'skirt' over your lampshade frame, working from the top down. Align each panel seam with a strut – don't worry too much if they are not exact as you can hide any misalignment with your trim. Start pinning at the end of a strut, pulling the fabric taut as you do this. Make sure you pin into the binding. Go round the top and bottom rings of the frame, repeating for each strut. Keep adding more pins, remembering each time to pull the fabric taut. Work around the frame re-pinning and stretching. Make sure you get rid of any puckering or creases as you go.

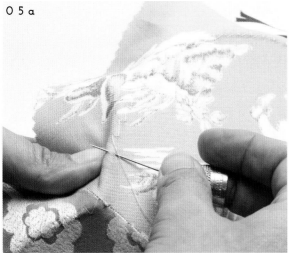

05a

05b

06a

06c

06b

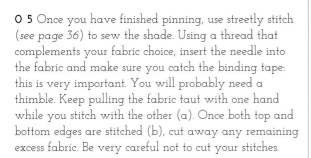

06d

0 5 Once you have finished pinning, use streetly stitch (*see page* 36) to sew the shade. Using a thread that complements your fabric choice, insert the needle into the fabric and make sure you catch the binding tape: this is very important. You will probably need a thimble. Keep pulling the fabric taut with one hand while you stitch with the other (a). Once both top and bottom edges are stitched (b), cut away any remaining excess fabric. Be very careful not to cut your stitches.

0 6 Use a wooden stirrer to apply glue to the reverse of the trim (a). Add the trim to the seam of each panel join by following the line of the strut, working from the top down. Once all the struts have been trimmed, add trim to the top ring of the shade (b). Make sure you cover up all visible stitching. Finally, add trim to the bottom ring of the shade (c, d). This will usually be some type of pompom, fringing or tassel trim. Attach the trim with the shade at eye level to ensure it is positioned correctly, and use pegs to hold it in place while the glue dries. You should now have a bespoke, boutique shade that is the belle of the ball. Turn the light on, grab a good book and enjoy!

FRAME TYPE: Retro reverse, double-scalloped

TECHNIQUE: Hand-stitched, multi-panelled, soft-sided, with integrated exterior lining and feature binding

PROJECT TIME: 8–10 hours

SKILL LEVEL: ♀ ♀ ♀ ♀ ♀

CLUB TARTAN

A GENTLEMAN'S HIGHLAND CLUB LAMPSHADE WITH A CONTEMPORARY TWIST

FABRIC & DECORATION

 tartan fabric of your choice, 2¼yd (2m). I've selected one that has a contemporary twist, but you might want something more traditional

 lining fabric, 2¼yd (2m). I'm using a fairly heavy-weight, slate-grey cotton

 black gimp, 5½yd (5m)

 dip-dyed 12in (30cm) fringing in grey and black, 2¼yd (2m)

TOOLS & MATERIALS

- black binding tape
- plump cushion
- brown paper
- marker pen
- paper scissors
- steam iron
- dressmaking pins
- tailor's chalk
- fabric scissors
- lills
- needle
- thimble
- bold thread
- fabric glue
- wooden stirrer
- pegs

01

01 Doing cheat panels (*see page 88*) or using two panels (*see page 78*) is all well and good, but working on the bias you won't be able to feature a patterned fabric with the pattern on the straight unless you hand stitch each panel. This is far more time consuming, but it does produce a beautiful finish and can make for a long-lasting shade. It is my favourite technique and very useful for tackling awkwardly shaped frames. Following the instructions on page 32, permanently bind the whole frame. In this case I have used black binding, as I want to make a feature of the exposed binding.

02

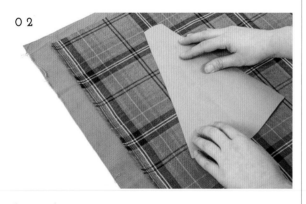

02 Using brown paper, create a template for each panel, as shown in the Frida Rocks project (*see page 88*). If the panels are of different shapes, you will need to create a number of templates. I am using a contemporary tartan fabric as the outer cover and a heavy, slate grey cotton for the lining. Iron the fabric well. Lay the fabrics on top of one another, wrong sides facing. Taking your first panel, move it around on top of the outer fabric to select the best part of the pattern. Work on the straight grain. Before you cut anything, make sure there is sufficient fabric to create panels with exactly the same pattern on them to cover the remaining panels. This is crucial.

TIP
If your fabric has a highly identifiable pattern, you will probably want to pattern match each panel. Bear this in mind as you position the paper template – this will also have a bearing on the amount of fabric you need.

03

03 Once you are happy with the position of the paper template, pin the template to your sandwiched fabric using dressmaking pins.

04

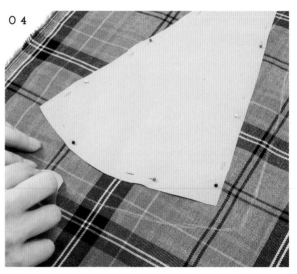

04 Draw round the template with tailor's chalk leaving approximately 2in (5cm) of fabric handling allowance.

0 5 Cut along your chalk line.

0 6 You now have your first panel of outer fabric and integrated exterior lining fabric. Put to one side, and follow the same process for each panel of your lampshade. Number them if necessary in order to identify their position on the frame. Iron the fabric again if necessary.

0 7 Take one piece of outer fabric and one piece of lining fabric, and sandwich them with the wrong sides facing together. If you have numbered the panels, you will need a corresponding panel of outer fabric and lining fabric.

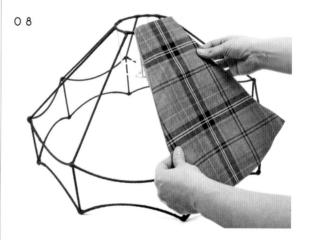

0 8 Lay the sandwiched fabric over the relevant panel of your frame. If you are pattern matching, pay particular attention to where you are positioning your fabric at this stage. You will need to replicate it for all the matching panels.

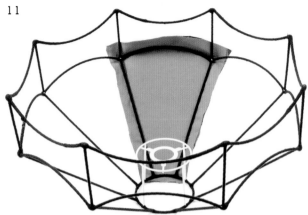

09 Pin out using lills. Begin at each of the four corners of the panel, and make sure you pin away from the frame. Keep both pieces of fabric taut as you do this. Be sure to pin through both pieces of fabric and the binding tape. Floating pins are of no use.

11 Check all the time that the lining fabric is as taut as the outer fabric. It can sometimes pucker if you change the tension on the fabric.

10 Continue to pin out evenly around the panel, stretching the fabric all the time. Be careful not to stretch the fabric to such an extent that it distorts the pattern shape.

12 Once the panel is fully pinned, go round once more re-pinning and stretching to make sure no part of the fabric is baggy. Make sure you are not distorting the pattern as you do this. There is a bit of an art to it and it does take time, but stick with it.

13 Stitch the panel using the streetly stitch (*see page 36*), removing the pins as you go.

15 Once your first panel is finished, continue working methodically around the shade attaching the rest of the panels.

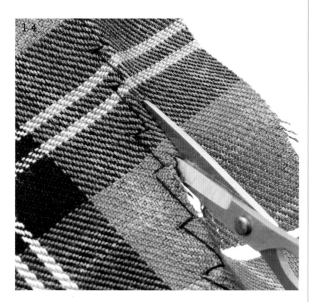

14 Trim the excess handling allowance as close to the shape of the panel as possible, without cutting any stitching by mistake. If you do cut a stitch by accident, stop cutting and restitch. You can use fabric or paper glue to fix stitching – put glue on your finger and run it along the stitching and any fraying fabric.

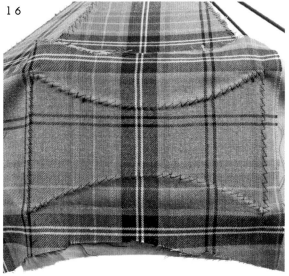

16 Remember to keep pattern matching as you move on to different-shaped panels.

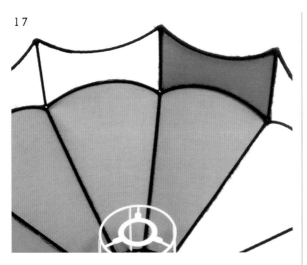

17 Check your lining all the time to make sure it's not puckering or gaping.

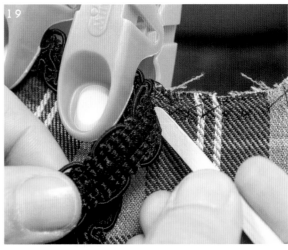

19 Attach trim to the top ring. I use pegs to hold the gimp in place while the glue dries. Remember to create an overlap at the end for a tidy finish. You will also need to run a line of gimp along the top ring of the gallery. The gallery is the intermediate ring where the top panels meet the bottom panels.

18 Starting with the struts, attach your trim. Work down from top to bottom ring. I am attaching gimp with glue applied with a wooden stirrer, but you could use a glue gun.

20 Attach your fringing to the bottom ring. Make sure your frame is at eye level while you do this, otherwise you risk positioning the trim too high up the frame. Glue the fringing, and hold it in place with pegs until the glue has dried.

2 1 Once the fringing glue has dried, run gimp around the bottom ring over the top of the fringing. Create a tidy overlap to finish.

💡 GET INSPIRED
Designer-makers creating truly beautiful lampshades using tartan and tweed include BeauVamp (*see page 162*) and Zoë Darlington (*see page 182*).

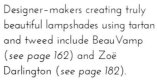

2 2

2 2 The Club Tartan lampshade is ready for business.

FRAME TYPE: Single-scalloped top and bottom ring

TECHNIQUE: Hard-sided decoupage using PVA glue

PROJECT TIME: 24 hours including drying time

SKILL LEVEL: 🔆 🔆 🔆 🔆 🔆

LA GITANA

A PATCHWORK OF VINTAGE SILKS, SARIS, KIMONO REMNANTS & FRENCH LINENS

FABRIC & DECORATION:

 lightweight white linen, 60in (1.5m)

 fabric remnants, approx. 2¼yd (2m) square; I have used a mixture of vintage silk scarves, kimono fabric, sari fabric, French linen and contemporary cottons

 grosgrain ribbon in a red wine colour, 3⅓yd (3m)

 tasselled fringing in a red wine colour, 60in (1.5m)

 braiding in a red wine colour, 40in (1m)

TOOLS & MATERIALS

- plump cushion
- brown paper
- marker pen
- paper scissors
- small coloured stickers
- self-adhesive lampshade PVC
- steam iron
- fabric scissors or pinking shears
- small embroidery scissors
- double-sided tape
- PVA glue
- mixing dish
- paintbrush
- wooden stirrer
- pegs

0 1 Follow steps 1 to 10 on pages 74–76 to make a basic hard-sided shade. Cover your laminated fabric in your choice of base fabric. It could be a neutral white, as I have used here. This will be decorated with decoupage – the term for using glue to apply paper and fabrics

0 3 Working on your base shade, take your first piece of fabric and decide where you are going to place it. Put some PVA glue in your mixing dish and use a paintbrush to apply a small amount evenly to the wrong side of the fabric piece and to the base shade. Stick the fabric on to the glued area of the shade, and smooth flat with the paintbrush. Any creases or bubbles in the fabric will affect the finish of your shade, so take your time. Try not to overload the fabric with glue, but do make sure it sticks fully.

0 2 Iron all your fabric, then cut into patches of different sizes. As an alternative, you can use pinking shears to create a zigzag edge. Plan a rough scheme with your choices of fabric. It's all about personal taste. You might want to sort fabrics by colour, or decide on a scheme for each individual panel.

> **TIP**
> Plasterers use PVA in vast quantities to seal walls, floors and ceilings before applying plaster. This is worth knowing because you can pick up large tubs of the glue very cheaply from hardware stores such as ScrewFix (www.screwfix.com) and Toolstation (www.toolstation.com). This is much more economical than most art supply retail outlets.

0 4 Work your way around the shade, applying PVA glue to each piece of fabric and sticking it in place to realise your original scheme. It's good for pieces to overlap the struts where the laminated PVC joins, as this will help strengthen your finished shade.

0 5 I'd suggest starting with any sheer or delicate fabrics, then placing thicker and more opaque fabrics on top of these. This will reduce show-through.

0 6 Keep working around the frame in this fashion, covering every white space.

0 7 Once the PVA has dried (I recommend allowing at least 12 hours for this, and ideally 24 hours), trim off any excess fabric from your top and bottom ring.

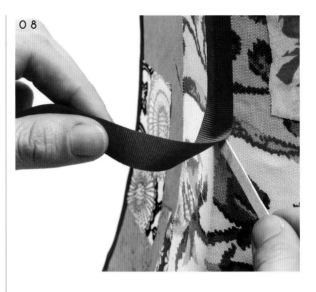

0 8 Working from the top down, add the trimming to the struts, using a wooden stirrer to apply small amounts of glue at a time.

0 9 To apply the trimming to the top ring, use the same method. Here, I peg the trim in place while the glue dries.

10 Apply the fringing to the bottom ring in the same way, using pegs to hold it in place.

TIPS

For decoupage, you can use any bits of fabric you have lying around. Old scarves, handkerchiefs and even vintage tablecloths work well. I have a box in my workroom where I put all the small leftover pieces of fabric after I finish a project. It's great to have a rummage in, to discover a real mix and match of fabrics. Seeing them in a new light will undoubtedly throw up new design ideas.

You could create a soft-sided shade as your base and then decoupage on to this. I would advise against PVA glue for this purpose though. Use a fabric spray adhesive instead, otherwise your base fabric may become distorted with the weight of the PVA glue.

11

11 The finished lampshade, with its decoupage decoration, will look spectacular.

💡 GET INSPIRED

Have a look at the incredible decoupage creations by Lisa Whatmough of Squint Limited (*see page 176*).

FRAME TYPE: *Bell*

TECHNIQUE: *Multi-panelled, soft-sided, hand-stitched, dip-dyed lampshade*

PROJECT TIME: *24 hours (including drying time)*

SKILL LEVEL: ♀ ♀ ♀ ♀ ♀

ALCHEMY: TATIANA

A DELICATE CANDY-FLOSS PINK AND ANTIQUE-GREY OMBRÉ PENDANT

FABRIC & DECORATION

white linen, 40in (1m) square

³/₈in (1cm) grey velvet ribbon, 3¹/₃yd (3m)

grey braid, 12in (30cm)

large, grey pompom fringing, 60in (1.5m)

TOOLS & MATERIALS

- plump cushion
- brown paper
- marker pen
- paper scissors
- dressmaking pins
- tailor's chalk
- fabric scissors
- cold-water fabric dyes in two colours
- wooden spoon
- measuring jug
- water
- bucket, large enough to submerge lampshade
- salt
- clothes rack
- metal hanger
- glue
- wooden stirrer
- pegs

0 1

0 1 Using the white linen, follow steps 1 to 14 on Club Tartan (*see pages 108–111*) to create a hand-stitched base cover. I have not lined this shade, so I'm only using one layer of fabric.

0 2

0 2 Mix your first colour of dye, following the manufacturer's guidelines. In this case, I am using flamingo-pink dye and I had to mix the contents of the sachet in 17fl oz (500ml) of warm water.

0 3 Stir the solution well, until the dye dissolves completely.

0 3

0 4 In a large bucket, pour in the recommended amount of water. In this case, I had to pour in at least six jugs of warm water.

0 4

0 7

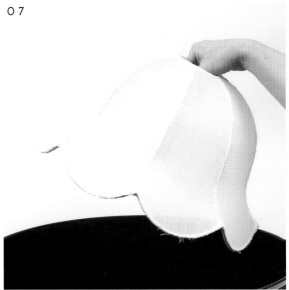

0 7 Now for the magic. Submerse your lampshade in the dye mixture. Make sure it is completely covered. Follow the manufacturer's instructions – I had to agitate the mixture for 15 minutes, and then leave the shade submerged for a further 45 minutes.

0 5

0 5 To the water, I added five tablespoons of household salt. Again, follow the dye manufacturer's guidelines.

0 6 Add your dissolved dye to the mix and stir well.

0 6

0 8

0 8 Once the time has elapsed, remove the shade from the mixture and put aside while you clean the bucket ready for the second dye colour. You can hang the lampshade over a bath while you do this. I use a clothes rack and a bent metal hanger to do this.

09

0 9 Prepare the second colour – in this case, an antique-grey dye – in the same way as the first. Always follow the manufacturer's guidelines.

1 0

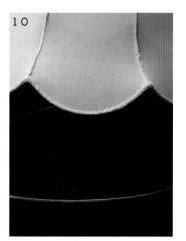

1 0 Calculate carefully how far up the shade you want the second colour to reach. This is the depth of dye mixture you should create. Submerge the shade in the dye mixture.

1 2

1 2 Once the time has elapsed, remove the shade from the bucket and hang it up to dry. It needs to be hung up overnight to make sure it is completely dry before you add any trimming.

1 1

1 1 Agitate according to the guidelines, then leave submerged for the recommended length of time. Here, it was approximately 45 minutes.

1 3

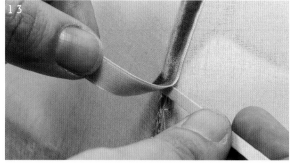

1 3 Attach the velvet ribbon to the struts, making sure to cover all the stitching. I have used glue here, applied with a wooden stirrer. Avoid loading the ribbon with too much glue, or it will seep out of the side of the ribbon and ruin the finish.

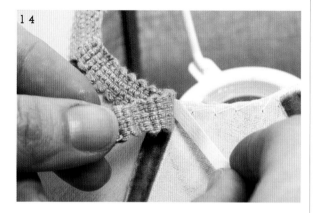

14 Apply the trim to the top ring in the same way.

15 Attach the trim to the bottom ring with the lampshade at eye level. As this shade is a pendant, position it temporarily on a table lamp base to do this. Use pegs to hold the trim in place while the glue dries, particularly if the trim is fairly heavy like these large pompoms.

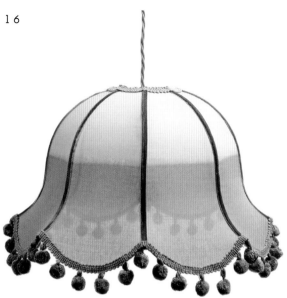

16 Your finished lampshade!

💡 GET INSPIRED

Designer-makers creating truly beautiful lampshades that feature ombré details include BeauVamp (see page 162). Have a look at Alice's beautiful work, and let it inspire your own creations.

FRAME TYPE: Half bowl/Tiffany

TECHNIQUE: Removable kitchen shade. (Called a kitchen shade, as they could be removed easily for washing, to remove grease and cooking smells.)

PROJECT TIME: 1 hour

SKILL LEVEL: 💡💡💡💡💡

MOLLY THE MOP CAP

A FUNKY REMOVABLE SHADE IN ORANGES & BROWNS, REMINISCENT OF THE 1970S

FABRIC & DECORATION

 lightweight fabric (I have used vintage barkcloth), 20in (50cm)

 ³⁄₈in (9mm) elastic, 60in (1.5m)

TOOLS & MATERIALS

- tape measure
- fabric scissors
- sewing machine
- steam iron
- safety pin for threading the elastic
- dressmaking pins

TIP
This is a great shade-making technique to apply to small candle half bowl / Tiffany frames. You could cover a number of them in contrasting fabrics and then attach them to a chandelier fitting.

01 Measure the circumference of the bottom ring of the frame, and add 5½in (14cm). Here, I used 48in (112cm) + 5½in (14cm) = 49½in (126cm).

03 Measure out 49½in (126cm) x 18½in (46.5cm). If you don't have a full width of fabric, measure two rectangles that are half the length plus ⅜in (1cm) for the seam. Here, the rectangles are 25¼in (64cm) by 18½in (46.5cm).

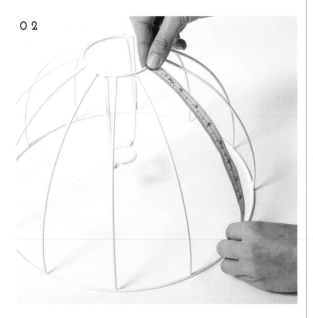

02 Measure from the top ring to the bottom ring, following the curve of the strut, and add 8in (20cm). Here, I used 10½in (26.5cm) + 8in (20cm) = 18½in (46.5cm).

04 Cut your fabric to size.

O 5 a

O 5 b

O 5 c

O 5 Sew the short sides of your rectangles together using a French seam, to create one continuous tube. To sew a French seam: stitch a single seam wrong sides together (a); cut and trim (b); then sew the right sides together (c).

O 6

O 6 Turn under the top edge of the fabric twice, to create a channel approximately $5/8$in (1.5cm) wide. Press and pin in place.

O 7

O 7 Stitch in place close to the folded edge to create the channel, leaving a $5/8$in (1.5cm) gap between the beginning and end of the stitch line to feed the elastic through.

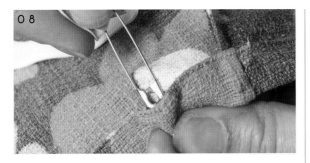

08 Using a safety pin, feed half the elastic through.

09 Make sure you secure both ends of the elastic.

10 On the bottom edge of the fabric, measure 7in (18cm) from the edge all the way around. Use pins to mark this.

11 Turn under ⅜–⅝in (1–1.5cm) along this bottom edge all the way around, and pin.

12 Bring the folded edge up to meet the pins used in Step 10, to create a channel approximately 3¼in (8cm) wide. Press and pin in place, and remove the guide pins.

13 Stitch in place close to the folded edge, leaving approximately ⅜in (1cm) gap between the beginning and end of the stitch line, in line with the gap on the top seam. This is to feed the elastic through.

1 4 Stitch parallel to this line, about ⅝in (1.5cm) from the first line (stitching through two layers of fabric) to create a channel. Stitch all the way around, allowing the end of the stitch line to overlap with the beginning of the stitch line. Thread the other half of the elastic through this channel and tie loosely in place.

1 5 Fit the lampshade cover over the frame.

1 6 Adjust the tightness of the elastic to suit the frame. Stitch the ends of the elastic in place and cut off the excess.

1 7 You have finished your Molly the Mop Cap marvel.

💡 GET INSPIRED
Polly Kettley of Folly & Glee contributed to this step-by-step tutorial. Have a look at her beautiful bark cloth creations on page 166.

FRAME TYPE: Straight Empire

TECHNIQUE: Pleated lampshade

PROJECT TIME: 7 hours

SKILL LEVEL: ♀ ♀ ♀ ♀ ♀

IKATA

A DELIGHTFUL, MINTY-FRESH PLEATED LITTLE NUMBER

FABRIC & DECORATION

Botanique by Joel Dewberry, 40in (1m) square

shot silk lining fabric, 40in (1m) square

white crocheted pompom fringing, 20in (50cm)

polka dot, aqua-coloured bias binding, 12in (30cm)

³/₈in (1cm) orange velvet ribbon, 40in (1m)

TOOLS & MATERIALS

- tape measure
- pencil
- steam iron
- ruler
- fabric scissors
- lills
- needle
- bold thread
- small embroidery scissors
- glue
- wooden stirrers
- pegs

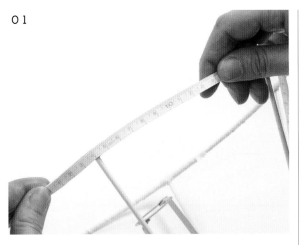

01

01 Traditionally, pleated shades have been made using sheer fabrics, but you can use any lightweight fabric. I am using cotton. This is a straight Empire shade, permanently bound top and bottom rings, and temporarily bound on two struts for the lining. To create the lining, go to basic techniques (*see page 38*). To make the pleated lampshade, first measure the circumference of the bottom ring, then multiply by three. Here, this is 3¼yd (96cm) x 3 = 9ft 6in (288cm). This is the length of fabric you will need to make this shade.

03

03 For this project I have used a 40in (1m) square of fabric and cut three panels out of it. The pleating must run on the straight grain not the bias, so pleats should run parallel to the selvedge. This is important. Iron your fabric to remove all creases, then measure the height carefully.

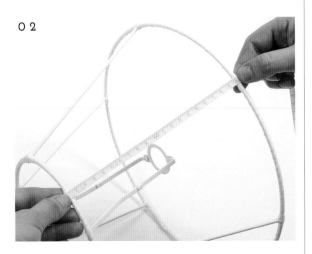

02

02 Determine the height by measuring a strut, then add 4in (10cm) for handling excess. Here, this is 8in (20cm) + 4in (10cm) = 12in (30cm). This is the height of fabric you will need.

04

04 Measure the width, then remove the selvedge.

0 5 Join all your measurements to create the first panel. Measure out the second and third panel in this manner.

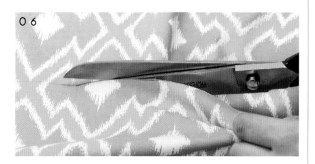

0 6 Cut out your three panels. Here, they measure 3ft 2in (96cm) wide by 1ft (30cm) high.

0 7 Make sure you pattern match if you are using a distinctive repeat, as I am doing here.

0 8 It is customary to pleat from right to left, and to start on the bottom ring. Determine how wide you want your pleats. I have selected approximately ³⁄₈in (1cm). You can measure them precisely if you want, but I prefer to do it by eye. Fold in the raw edge of the short side of your first panel by ³⁄₈in (1cm). The fabric should be right side out.

0 9 Starting at the bottom ring where the strut meets the ring, pin the folded fabric with a 2in (5cm) handling excess below the bottom ring. Keep this handling excess as uniform as possible, as you work around the frame.

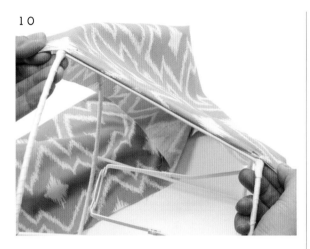

10 Pulling the folded fabric taut, run it up along the strut and pin the first pleat to the top ring.

12 Fold a second pleat over this gap.

11 Working solely on the bottom ring now, leave a gap approximately twice the width of the first pleat.

13 Pin and work your way around the bottom strut, creating pleats and pinning until you get to the next strut. Stop here. I have created 11 pleats per panel, but this number may vary. However, you should have the same number of pleats for each panel and the pleats should be as uniform as possible.

14

14 When you are happy with the spacing of your pleats along the bottom ring of the first panel (some adjustments may be needed), you can start pinning pleats along the top ring. In this case, the frame has a smaller top ring so the spacing between each pleat will be smaller and there may be some overlapping of fabric. Make sure you pin fabric out, so it is as taut as possible. Be sure to pin through both fabric and binding tape. Floating pins are of no use to anyone.

15

15 Once both top and bottom ring pleats have been pinned for the first panel, you can hand sew the fabric to the binding tape using the streetly stitch (*see page 36*). Do not sew the top or bottom of your first pleat, though. This must remain pinned, as you will need to lift this when you arrive at your last pleat. Be sure to sew through the fabric and the binding tape.

16

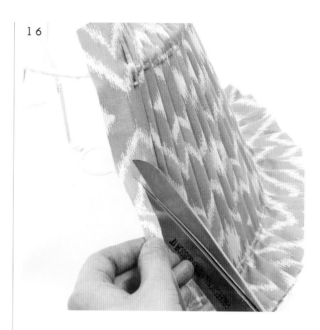

16 Work around the frame in this way, pleating, pinning and sewing one panel at a time. In this case, each length of fabric works across two panels. When you run out of fabric, leave double the width of a pleat, ³⁄₄in (2cm). Trim any excess fabric off.

17

17 Take a new piece of fabric and fold over the raw edge by ³⁄₈in (1cm).

18 Then, lay this over the previous piece of fabric to create a ³⁄₈in (1cm) pleat. Pin as you did previously, and continue pleating around the frame – adding additional fabric panels as and when you need them.

19 When you arrive back at your first pleat, your shade should look something like this.

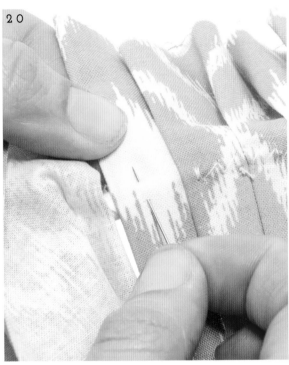

20 Remove the pin from your very first pleat on the bottom ring.

21 Trim any excess fabric off your final pleat, to leave it measuring ³⁄₄in (2cm) all the way from the bottom ring to the top ring.

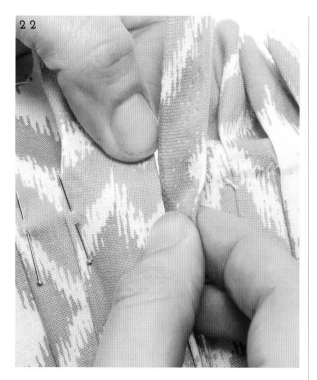

2 2 Lift the very first pleat up, and slip the last pleat underneath it.

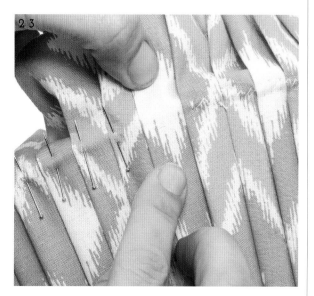

2 3 Fold the first pleat back down and make sure that the last pleat is approximately ³⁄₈in (1cm), to match the rest of the pleats.

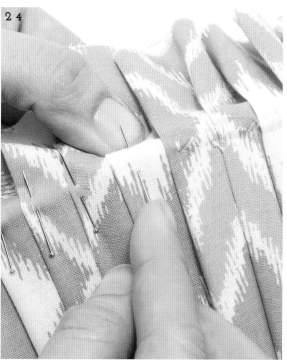

2 4 Repin the final pleat. Now, follow the same method on the top ring. Sew any remaining pleats to the binding tape.

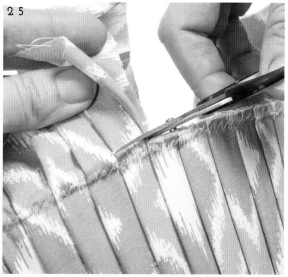

2 5 When everything is stitched, you can trim back all the excess fabric. Be very careful not to cut into your stitching, as this will create baggy pleats.

26

26 The finished, pleated outer cover is ready to be lined. Follow the steps on page 41 to do this, then return here to add the trim.

28

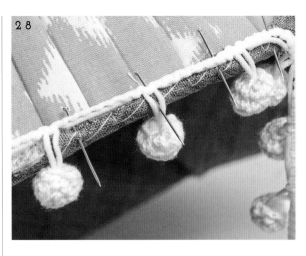

28 In this instance, I am going to stitch the pompom fringing on as it is rather too thin to glue. First, pin out the pompom fringing all around the bottom ring to hold it in place. Do this at eye level, by putting the lampshade on a lamp base.

27

27 Once the lining has been inserted, and the gimbal tidies attached, add the bias binding to the top ring so that it covers the area where the lining is stitched over the outer cover. I use glue applied with a wooden stirrer and pegs to hold the bias binding in place while the glue dries.

29

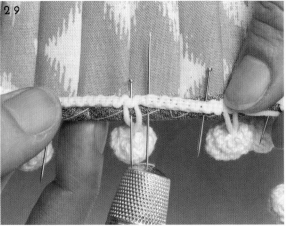

29 I have used the streetly stitch again here to sew the pompoms on, just a mini version of it.

3 0 Glue the orange velvet trim along the bias binding on the top ring, so that it overlaps it slightly. This will require a steady hand to keep it straight. Use pegs to hold the ribbon in place while the glue dries.

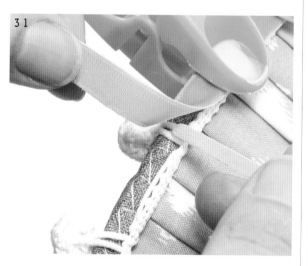

3 1 Finally, glue the orange ribbon along the bottom ring to cover up the stitching. Use pegs here, too, to hold the ribbon in place while the glue dries. When everything is dry, remove the pegs.

3 2 Your pleated lampshade is complete.

> **TIP**
> You could use vintage linen to pleat with and then dip dye following the steps on page 120. This can look very effective and is a great way to upcycle a slightly worn vintage tablecloth.

FRAME TYPE: Collar top

TECHNIQUE: Swathed lampshade

PROJECT TIME: 9 hours

SKILL LEVEL: ♀ ♀ ♀ ♀ ♀

FLAMING JUNO

A FLAMBOYANT STATEMENT PIECE IN A FIERY ORANGE AND TEAL

FABRIC & DECORATION

orange taffeta, 60in
(1.5m) square

teal feather trimming,
40in (1m)

teal gimp, 40in (1m)

TOOLS & MATERIALS

- binding tape
- tape measure
- pencil
- ruler
- fabric scissors
- steam iron
- lills
- needle
- thread
- thimble
- glue
- wooden stirrer
- pegs

O 1 Bind the top and bottom rings. I am using a collar top frame, so I have also bound the ring of the collar. To determine how much fabric you are going to need, measure the circumference of the bottom ring and multiply this by three to give you the length of fabric needed. In this case, it is 31½in (80cm) x 3 = 94½in (240cm). You may need to use several panels of fabric.

O 3 Lay out your fabric face down on your work surface. It is important that you work on the straight grain of the fabric. You need to be in alignment with the selvedge. Mark out your panel height, which in this case is 15in (38cm).

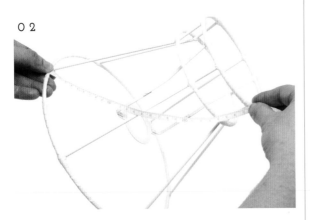

O 2 Measure from the base of one strut where it meets the bottom ring, to the top of the next strut but one, where it meets the top ring. Make sure you skip a strut, and use a tape measure to mimic the swathed line not a completely straight line. Add around 2in (5cm) to the top and bottom of your measurement (4in [10cm] in total) as handling allowance. This is the height of fabric you need. In this case, it is 11in (28cm) plus 4in (10cm) = 15in (38cm).

O 4 Mark out your panel length, which in this case is 31½in (80cm). Make sure you work at least 1½in (2cm) in from the selvedge.

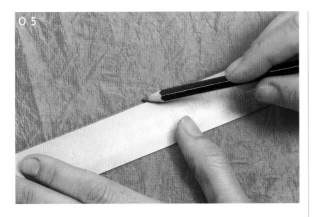

0 5 You are going to cut three panels of 31½in (80cm) x 15in (38cm) out of the fabric. On each panel, mark halfway along the length, in this case 15¾in (40cm). This is the amount of fabric you will have to swathe between two struts. The frame I am working with has six struts and therefore six panels, so each of the three cut pieces of fabric will work across two panels.

0 6 Cut the selvedge off.

0 7 Cut out your three panels, and iron. The beauty of taffeta is that it retains a soft, crushed look, so excessive ironing isn't required.

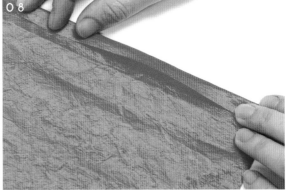

0 8 Lay out the first of the three lengths of fabric, right side down. Fold over a seam of ⅜in (1cm) on one of the short ends.

0 9

0 9 Turn the fabric over so it is right side up. Using both hands, stretch the fabric from the bottom ring at a join with a strut, up to the top of the next strut but one. Make sure you leave a 2in (5cm) handling allowance top and bottom.

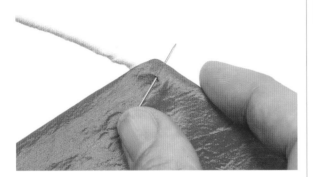

10 Start pinning out your swathed shade on the bottom ring at the join with a strut. The convention is to pleat from right to left, turning the shade as you go.

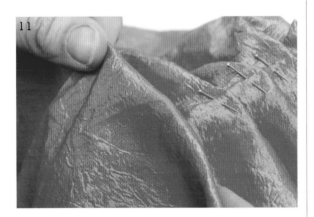

11 I am creating approximately ³⁄₈in (1cm) pleats. You will need to leave a gap of double this, ³⁄₄in (2cm), before you start the next pleat, and so on. You must maintain the 2in (5cm) handling allowance throughout the pleating process, or you may run out of fabric.

12 Pin out the whole panel along the bottom ring, creating even pleats as you go. Once you have reached the 15³⁄₄in (40cm) mark – in other words, the fabric allowance for that panel – you will know how many pleats you can fit to a panel. You may have to adjust your pleating and pinning to get this even. In this case, I have made ten pleats per panel.

13 Once the bottom of the panel is done, move on to the top ring. It is very important that you remember to skip a strut in order to create the swathed effect.

1 5 Once you have pinned one panel top and bottom, oversew using the streetly stitch (*see page 36*). It is important not to sew your very first pleat. Leave this pinned. I have used white thread here for visibility's sake, but it is best to match the colour of thread to the fabric. Hold the fabric as taut as possible while you sew. The last thing you want is baggy pleats.

1 4 Start to pin out the fabric on the top ring, remembering to create the same number of pleats as the bottom ring and to use up all the fabric allowance for the panel. As the top ring is a lot smaller than the bottom ring on this frame, the pleats will be smaller and there will be more overlapping of fabric.

1 6 Keep checking to make sure you've sewn all the way through to the binding tape, particularly on the top ring, as you have a lot of layers of fabric to get through.

17

17 Once you have pleated two panels, you will have run out of fabric. So, start with the second piece. Trim any excess fabric from your first piece, leaving at least ³⁄₄in (2cm) allowance.

18

18 Take your second piece of 31¹⁄₂in (80cm) x 15in (38cm) fabric. As you did at the beginning, fold over a seam of ³⁄₈in (1cm).

19

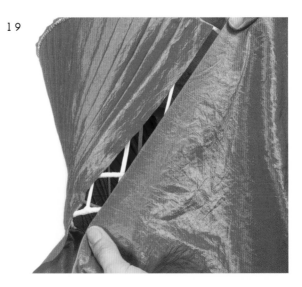

19 Turn the fabric right side up.

20

20 Using both hands, lay the new piece of fabric across the bottom and top rings. Ensure the handling allowance of 2in (5cm) top and 2in (5cm) bottom is kept even. Starting with the bottom ring again, leave a ³⁄₈in (1cm) space from the last pleat you created.

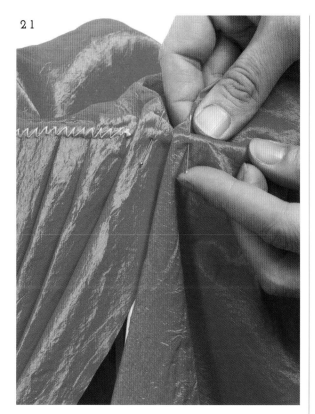

2 1 Pin the first pleat of the new piece of fabric to the bottom ring, and follow steps 11 to 16 once more.

2 2 You can see here how the swathing is starting to look. Continue to work around the frame until you have pleated every panel.

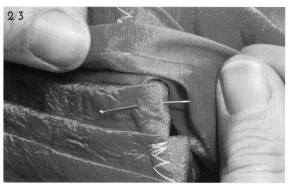

2 3 You should eventually arrive back at your very first pleat.

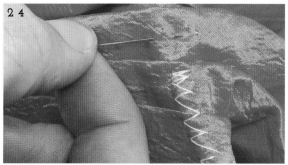

2 4 Remove the pin from your first pleat on the bottom ring.

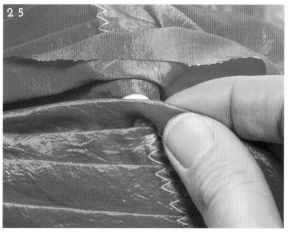

2 5 Trim any excess fabric off your final pleat, to leave it measuring ³/4in (2cm) all the way from the bottom ring to the top ring.

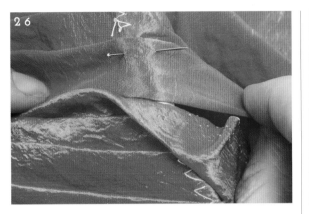

2 6 Lift the first pleat up and slip the last pleat underneath it.

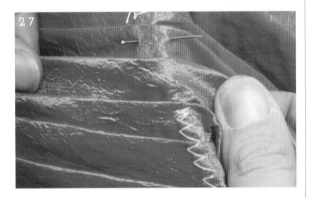

2 7 Fold the first pleat back down and make sure the last pleat is approximately 3/8in (1cm) to match the rest of the pleats.

2 8 Repin the final pleat. Follow the same process on the top ring. Then oversew any remaining pleats to the binding tape.

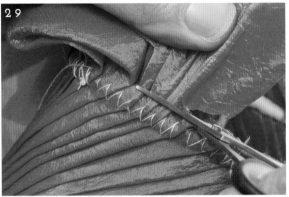

2 9 When everything is stitched, trim all the excess fabric back. Be very careful not to cut into your stitching. If you do, restitch immediately.

3 0

3 0 The finished, swathed shade is ready for trimming. If you wish to add lining, now is the time to do it. Follow the steps on page 41 to do this, then return here to add the trim.

3 1 To add the feathered trim, apply glue with a wooden stirrer. I am not using pegs here to hold it in place while the glue dries, as the pegs would distort the shape of the feathers. Instead I am using lills.

> **TIP**
> Taffeta is a surprisingly robust fabric, so I chose not to line this shade. If you are using a sheer fabric, I would recommend lining.

3 2 Add the gimp to the top ring using glue applied with a wooden stirrer. Here I have used pegs to secure the trim in place while the glue dries.

3 3 Tidy up the feather trim with gimp, attaching it with glue and a wooden stirrer.

3 4

3 4 The flamboyant finished shade is one of my favourites.

FRAME TYPE: Any

TECHNIQUE: Reconditioning, repurposing, reinventing, revisiting a lamp base

PROJECT TIME: Variable. In this case 2 hours, not including time for professional rewiring

SKILL LEVEL: ♀ ♀ ♀ ♀ ♀

ALL ABOUT THE BASE

THE FINISHING TOUCHES

FABRIC & DECORATION

vintage find or dilapidated lamp base in need of love and attention

Circa cotton fabric by Jennifer Paganelli, 40in (1m) square

oversized pompom fringing in bubblegum pink, 40in (1m)

³⁄₈in (10mm) magenta velvet ribbon, 20in (50cm)

TOOLS & MATERIALS

- household cleaning wipes
- sandpaper: medium (60–80 grit), fine (100–120 grit), very fine (150–220 grit), depending on the amount of tidying up needed
- cotton buds
- acetone/nail polish remover
- cloth, bowl and washing-up liquid
- masking tape
- paintbrush
- primer: I tend to use Autentico chalk paint, as I regularly upstyle furniture
- hair dryer
- matt black spray paint

0 1 You can paint them, strip them, distress them ... there are so many things you can do to a lamp base if you have a little vision. Look beyond first impressions. I've picked up many overlooked lamp bases and transformed them with a little bit of lateral thinking into unique pieces. This is a lamp base and shade I purchased for very little money. It was love at first sight, but it did look a little neglected. I removed the shade and put this aside for later.

0 2 The first thing to do is to give the base a good clean. I use household wipes for this purpose.

0 3 The base had nubby bits of paint and other uneven elements on the surface, so I lightly sanded it all over with a fine-grit sandpaper. Don't use a coarse sandpaper as this will sand away all the details!

0 4 To get dirt out of the small corners, I used a cotton bud and some nail polish remover.

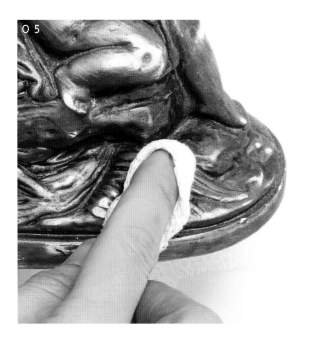

0 5

0 5 Once you're satisfied that your base is free of any residue, wipe it down with a cloth dipped in warm water and washing-up liquid. Make sure the cloth is not wringing wet.

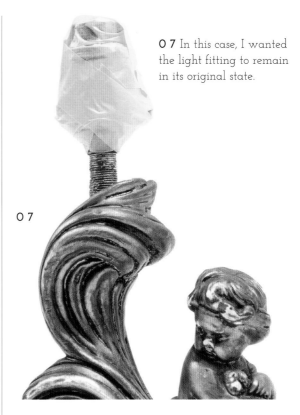

0 7 In this case, I wanted the light fitting to remain in its original state.

0 7

0 6

0 6 Using masking tape, mask any areas you do not want to be painted.

0 8

0 8 Apply your primer. In this case I am using Autentico chalk paint in Vanille. Do not overload the paintbrush. It only needs one light coat, but do make sure you get good coverage and don't miss any spots.

09

09 I use a hair dryer to speed up the drying time. If you are not using chalk paint, do read the manufacturer's instructions carefully on how to apply the primer and the length of time it needs to dry.

10

10 Once the primer is completely dry, you can have fun spray painting. Do this in a well-ventilated place. I use my garden. Read the manufacturer's instructions before you start. Always hold the can about 12in (30cm) from the base. It is better to apply two fine coats than one heavy coat of paint. Too much paint in one go can cause the paint to pool and run, making the finish uneven and streaky.

11

11 Leave the base to dry.

12

12 Once the paint has dried completely, remove the masking tape.

13

13 You can now turn your attention to the shade. I stripped this one, gave it a good clean, and bound the top and bottom rings (*see page 32*). I then re-covered it following the steps on pages 78–87.

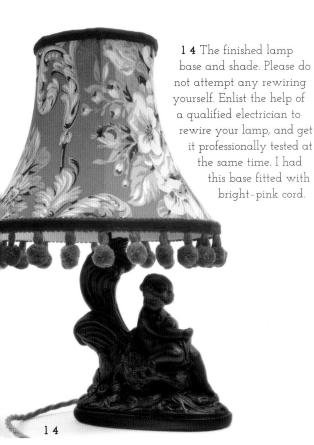

14 The finished lamp base and shade. Please do not attempt any rewiring yourself. Enlist the help of a qualified electrician to rewire your lamp, and get it professionally tested at the same time. I had this base fitted with bright-pink cord.

14

A NOTE ABOUT PROPORTION

There is a vast range of lamp bases available in all shapes and sizes. You can also transform old vases and candlesticks into lamp bases with a little imagination. Polly Kettley of Folly & Glee has repurposed glass decanters and created beautiful lamp bases as a result (*see page 166*). Choose your lamp base wisely, as the wrong base matched with the wrong shade can create a very uncomfortable lighting solution. Be aware that too spindly a base will easily tip over with a shade attached. I prefer a solid base and one that has a bit of character too. However, you don't want base and shade vying for attention so I would always recommend pairing a solid-coloured base with a busy shade and vice versa.

There are some general rules:

- The height of the shade should be about ⁵⁄₈ the height of the base.
- The diameter of the bottom ring of your lampshade should be roughly ⁴⁄₅ of the height of the base.
- The lampshade should not look top heavy.
- The bottom ring of the shade should hang about 2in (5cm) below the light fitting on the base.

I am a great believer that rules are made to be broken, so go with your instinct. Mix and match to see what works for you, for the space you are working in, and for the overall 'look' you are after.

💡 **GET INSPIRED**
Designer-makers creating truly beautiful lamp bases include Abigail Ahern (*see page 160*) and Mineheart (*see page 172*).

LEADING LIGHTS

In this chapter, we illuminate the work of 12 designer-makers to show you that there are no limits to what can be achieved when making and designing lampshades. These creatives have taken the humble lampshade to new heights. They all champion the lampshade in a distinctive manner, and understand the importance of light in the home and in public spaces. We feature names that are both well known and up and coming, to show the breadth of what can be achieved. They all share a passion for designing lampshades, working with bases and surface patterns, and manipulating fabric. Explore Abigail Ahern's kooky animal bases; Squint Limited's opulent decoupage lampshades; Rockville's love of polkadots and fringing; BeauVamp's eclectic use of fabrics; Zoë Darlington's belief in harnessing traditional techniques; Lampara's collaboration with surface print designers; Mineheart's witty lighting solutions-come-art pieces; Boris Design Studio's modern take on humble felt; Timorous Beasties' boundary-pushing surface patterns; Folly & Glee's and Made by Sally Whiting's celebration of vintage fabrics, and Swee Mei's passion for oriental-inspired design. You're sure to find inspiration for your own work.

Designer, style maven, author, TV presenter, retailer and blogger, Abigail Ahern is recognized among design aficionados for her enchanting take on interiors. Her London-based emporium has been voted one of the coolest places to shop by *Elle Decoration* and stocks the eponymous Abigail Ahern label as well as an ever-changing collection of vintage finds sourced from far and wide. I discovered her work when I fell in love with her signature dog lamps.

ABIGAIL AHERN

www.abigailahern.com

After working for Terence Conran's publishing house for six years, Abigail relocated to the USA and trained as a designer through a correspondence course. She returned to the UK in the early 2000s, and opened her atelier in London. After a few years sourcing products from around the globe, she saw the possibilities in lighting. She began creating her own lamp designs, and had them made by a small group of artisans in Paris. With a growing following, Abigail's statement lamps flew off the shelves and garnered justifiable attention from the design press.

'Nobody was at the time making lamps that were beautifully crafted, but also a little whimsical and tongue in cheek... I've been lucky that my work has been picked up by the press since our very early days, so marketing has never been much of a problem.'

Abigail's love of tactile materials and the unexpected is apparent immediately. She designs with taffeta, velvet, Indian marble, French textiles and ceramics in mind. 'I'm rubbish at sketching, unfortunately! I see ideas in my head, which I then sort of pull together via a very rough sketch and mood board.' Her notebook of ideas and the computer are indispensable to the way in which she designs. 'I also have a giant artwork of Superman on the wall of my studio, and he inspires me to keep going!'

'The stands are an essential part of my lighting. I design them, and then they're made by a small British factory that specializes in beautiful ceramics.'

Combining classic with contemporary style, BeauVamp creates original and vintage-inspired fabric lighting, shaking up tradition with a twist and offering a completely tailor-made design and consultation service personal to your own tastes and requirements. All lampshades are hand-crafted using original vintage fabrics, handwoven silks and designer textiles, finished with an abundance of luxurious trimmings. A selection of hand-turned and exclusively designed lamp stands is also available in an assortment of speciality woods and come in a range of finishes to suit your lampshade.

BEAUVAMP

www.beauvamp.com

With a background in the events and hospitality industry as a creative development manager proposing theme and design ideas to corporate clients, Alice Moylan – the creative force behind BeauVamp – wanted to be more hands on designing and making for herself and others. 'It's always been in my nature to be creative and I started breathing new life into second-hand furniture as a bit of a hobby, but when I got hooked on it, I realised that it may be possible to turn it into a business.' With this in mind, Alice enrolled onto a local furniture and upholstery course where she learnt all sorts of renovation techniques. Her favourite project by far was salvaging an old lampshade and stand and the rest, as they say, is history. 'I knew then and there that lamps were going to be my thing as I got to experiment with fabrics as well as restoring the wood. I completely loved the transformation and was hooked.'

Equipped with an abundance of new-found knowledge and fuelled by a passion for making and creativity, BeauVamp was officially born in 2006. Alice freely admits that a lot of her lampshade-making techniques have been self-taught, combined with the generosity of other lampshade makers working in the industry who have shared some valuable pieces of information over the years. She now has a comprehensive portfolio of lampshade designs that she sells through a number of online stockists, including her own website with online shop. She has further

developed the BeauVamp brand by working on commercial and interior design projects, and her work has been featured on TV.

Alice juggles running BeauVamp with motherhood, getting the kids to school in the morning after which point her 'working' day begins. Once emails have been attended to, she'll take a look at her project list and start to prepare for orders before turning her head to the hands-on 'make' time. Alice will craft lampshades until mid afternoon, by which point she needs to make her priority list for the next day and answer any further emails that have come in. She also finds time for PR work. It's a busy lifestyle, but one that she thrives on. Asked what motivates her each day, Alice says, 'doing something I love every day as a job whilst being my own boss is just brilliant.'

RIGHT *Alice has recently collaborated with textile designer Jody Myerscough-Walker from Bon. This is the BonWave lampshade.*

Katarina Ivarsson and Anna Karlsson founded Boris Design Studio after working together at SWE DES, a joint venture in Hong Kong by Sweden's leading design consultancies. Blending Scandinavian design heritage and creativity with a very hands-on approach, they believe in sustainability and are convinced that great ideas are born from curiosity. They are based in Hong Kong, and the Grandma shade is one of their most successful products; it is made from felt and 100 per cent sustainable materials.

BORIS DESIGN STUDIO

www.borisdesignstudio.com

What if you could send a lampshade in an envelope instead of a container? This was the starting point for Boris Design Studio. 'We wanted to create voluminous shades that could be transported in a better way, without wasting space, and by that saving energy and resources. What we did was create a series of voluminous light shades that fold totally flat due to their smart pattern construction and therefore take up minimum space during transportation. By using felt as the main material we also eliminated several steps in the production, as the material does not need any edge treatments or stabilization coatings. After cutting and stamping out the pattern sections, they are simply stitched together by hand and then we have a ready shade. There are unlimited possibilities for mixing materials, colours and patterns with different cord combinations.'

They describe their favourite approach to work as 'dirty prototyping'. They make all the prototypes and development samples themselves, but for production they use a small team of seamstresses. 'We like to be hands on and get an understanding of how things really work. While talking about an idea we make it grow, and by trying it out in paper or fabric, adding a few stitches or glue, we make it come to life. Don't underestimate the power of dirty prototyping to try out new ideas – a glue gun and some cardboard can take you far in the design process.'

Katarina and Anna are passionate about materials and have built up a wonderful library of materials and samples. The Boris philosophy is to source sustainable materials that are renewable, recycled and eco-smart. Based in Hong Kong, they have very good access to suppliers. 'We love to work with textures. I think you can say textures and sustainability are our signature elements.'

  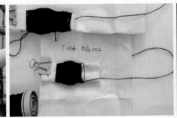 

ABOVE *The nostalgic shades — Anna Barbara, Hildur and Brita — are inspired by, and named after, Katarina and Anna's grandmas.*

The large shade is the Anna Barbara, a flamboyant Grandma from the East. A voluptuous shade that makes a fantastic centrepiece, it fits well over a dining table.

The medium shade is the Hildur, a shapely Grandma from the North. A classic curvy shade with a lot of character, it makes a statement in any room.

The smallest shade is the Brita, an elegant Grandma from the South. This timeless shade is highly versatile within the home.

Since 2010, Folly & Glee has been on a mission to revive, repurpose and revamp lighting. Polly Kettley is the creative brains behind the company, and her signature style is original, mid-century, cotton bark cloths that she sources from all over the world. Folly & Glee's copper-wire frames are made exclusively in Sussex, England, in every shape and dimension imaginable.

FOLLY & GLEE

www.follyandglee.co.uk

The origins of Polly's work were a stack of 1970s craft magazines bought at auction, in which she discovered basic instructions for both rigid and tailored lampshades. 'I couldn't wait to have a go, but finding the rings, frames and tape proved almost impossible. There were none of the kits available then. My first attempts to re-cover existing lampshades with a hotchpotch of glue and masking tape were not pretty!'

When Polly first began looking for vintage fabric at jumble sales, she found one particular piece that she thought was a slubby linen. Once she started looking for more, she discovered it was bark cloth — and it was love at first sight. 'The wonderful nubby texture and intensity of colour just can't be replicated by modern fabrics.' Fed up with never being able to find sufficient trimmings that complemented the depth of colour achieved on bark cloth, Polly started

hand dyeing her own organic cotton fringes and braids. She has also repurposed vintage colanders and jelly moulds, fashioned table lamps from crystal decanters, and made floor lamps from wooden shoe lasts.

Folly & Glee's lampshades match frame and fabric to capture the mood of a particular era. 'With the 1970s Pop Art prints, I love to do really tall cones. The 1930s florals suit traditional scalloped and bowed frames, and the Eames era prints make fabulous drums. Often a particular fabric will inspire a new design. My wire technician is fantastic — with over 40 years' experience of frame making he can do pretty much anything. My most recent example is our very popular Vetebrod frame, so called because of its Swedish heritage and resemblance to the traditional sweet loaf made from cardamom.'

ADVICE FOR THE NOVICE MAKER
'Be crystal clear about who your market is and what they want. With that firmly in mind, ensure you have a unique offering, whether it be your choice of fabric and trimmings, the frame shapes and sizes you work with or the technique you use: for example, pleating, patchwork.'

FOLLY
&
GLEE

With
Love

Lampara, launched in 2013, is the creative brainchild of Diane Wilson, and was born from a love of textile and pattern design. Diane's aim is to curate an inspiring collection, and she collaborates with a range of designers to create a striking and beautifully eclectic mix of lampshades. All of the lampshades are digitally printed in the UK on 100 per cent cotton with a 100% cotton contrast interior.

LAMPARA

www.lampara.co.uk

Diane studied at Bradford Art College, where she was strongly influenced by the history of the textile mills of Yorkshire, England, and regular visits to Salts Mill, Saltaire (an old textile mill now converted into the David Hockney gallery). After a career in publishing, she 'decided to go back to my roots and get out some old books on pattern design, which re-ignited a passion for design and textiles.' At the time she hadn't identified her product of choice, but a three-week business course resulted in literally a 'light bulb' moment — lampshades.

Diane found a gap in the market when she was trying to find homewares. 'I love colour and I was finding homewares really quite boring. I had been looking for large drum lampshades online and could only find plain-coloured shades. I decided that the lampshade could be like a "frame" and would be a great way of displaying contemporary design.'

Lampara produces handmade drum lampshades and matching cushions that are bursting with colour. It has featured the work of innovative and boundary-pushing contemporary designers including Sarah Arnett, Nadia Taylor, Oliver Goddard, Kate Gabb, Isabel Crossman, DanYell, Beki Gowing, Ailsa Munro, Katrina Voloder and Ana Montiel.

PHILSOPHY

'The business ethos is about promoting UK design and manufacture. It is much more expensive to print here but after studying Art in the city of Bradford and seeing the textile industry practically die, I decided that I wanted to be part of reviving the UK's textile industry.'

LEFT *Diane regularly collaborates with established and emerging talent in the UK, producing a diverse range of lampshades.*

Lampshade maker, crafter and fabric collector, Sally Whiting works out of an idyllic seafront studio – called Margot – on the Sussex coast of England, which she shares with fellow makers Louise Tyler, Melanie Barnes (geoffreyandgrace), and Ellie Bond (I AM ELLIE BOND). The majority of Sally's work is bespoke one-offs. She has a steady flow of commissions, which she supplements with her popular workshops. Sally will turn her hand to any lampshade-making technique and is always on the lookout for creative challenges.

MADE BY SALLY WHITING

www.facebook.com/madebysallywhiting

Made by Sally Whiting is 'a little golden beach hut makery – Margot – with a big handmade heart.' Sally studied for a degree in Textiles and Surface Pattern, and has a lifelong passion for vintage fabrics. Her first lampshade revamp was inspired by Tif Fussell and Rachelle Blondel's book *Granny Chic* – a fun and very simple stick, glue, patch and piece approach to lampshade restoration. 'When you are gluing over the top of a plain lampshade that you have picked up from a charity shop, there really is no right or wrong way.'

Sally soon learned how to cover a drum shade, and was inspired by three beautiful books from the 1960s that featured diagrams and instructions on making lampshades. She opened her home to the local art trail to show what she had been creating, and began running workshops at her local sewing shop, More Sewing. She combined this with selling at local craft and vintage fairs.

Inspired by these traditional techniques, Sally started to create and make different sizes and shapes of shades, dipping into her vast collection of pre-loved fabrics from the 1950s to early 1980s.

RIGHT *Sally's very popular fairy lights are made from beautiful vintage silk scarves.*

'Keep going, you never know which direction it's going to take you.'

Mineheart — the home of eccentric British design — was founded in 2010 by Anglo-Italian design duo Brendan Young and Vanessa Battaglia. Both are product and interior designers known for their playful approach to design and innovative use of materials and imagery. Their designs include the striking Sistine pendant light.

MINEHEART

www.mineheart.com

Although disinclined to attach any kind of signature style to their work, Brendan and Vanessa do identify the recurring theme of re-appropriation. Much of their inspiration comes from old things and memories of the past, particularly the Renaissance period.

Once an idea has been given the green light, there is no set process — each product is different and is born in a different way. The Sistine lampshade, for example, was an extremely simple idea. First, they sketched some collage-style visuals of the shade using images by Michelangelo on the diffuser. After a few weeks pinned on the wall of ideas, they selected a few favourites to make into prototypes. When the prototype shade arrived, it was installed in the studio and they lived with it for a while.

'In this case we felt the imagery needed a slightly more modern edge, so we commissioned Himitsuhana, a very talented Italian photographer and digital artist who creates amazing photos that look like paintings. She produced a few proposals for us and eventually we chose this one with three maidens floating around a dove.'

RIGHT *The Sistine pendant light is inspired by frescoes and chapel ceilings. An elegantly proportioned, circular shade supports a diffuser featuring an image of three sisters floating in the sky around a dove. The halo of light around the dove is positioned directly below the light source, so that light emanates from the dove.*

Rockville, based in East Sussex, England, was founded in 2011 by Charlotte Elfdahl. It was born from the idea of not having very much but wanting what you have to be extra special. The result is something a little bit unexpected, yet familiar and reassuring. The website Home of Rockville is essential viewing for all lampshade lovers.

ROCKVILLE

www.homeofrockville.co.uk

It was not until Charlotte bought her first property, a Victorian seaside apartment, that she started to really think about domestic lighting. 'The rooms were big and I just could not find any suitable lighting until I came across an old standard lamp with a tatty shade in a charity shop and fell in love. I loved the subdued light it spread as well as the iconic shape and the human scale.'

Charlotte went on to learn the craft of making lined-fabric lampshades at Metropolitan University in London before founding Rockville. She has worked with an array of fabrics, colours, finishes and frame shapes. Her signature style has evolved into the double-scalloped frame with a pelmet, set on the standard lamp stands she loves. 'All the lamp stands I picked up at charity shops were different heights and different colours. As I felt this was distracting from the quality of the shades, I decided to unify the lamps by painting them all the same colour. As time went

on I realized I could not rely on finding lamps in second-hand shops anymore so I decided to have my own standard lamps made and have them turned locally for me off site.'

Charlotte credits the humble thimble as the most invaluable tool when making shades. 'The pins are essential too. I use the short dressmaking pins in steel as these bend less easily than any of the longer pins. Upholstery thread helps and is strong enough to withstand pulling; and, finally, a sharp pair of tailor's scissors are crucial to shear the fabric as close to the frame as possible.'

One of Charlotte's proudest moments was being asked by Tibro Centre of Crafts in Sweden to teach lampshade making to their upholstery students. 'The fellow craft teachers there were so proud of their respective trades and this is when I realized I was now a practising craftsperson myself, something that had not occurred to me before.'

'My first lampshade was a small Empire-shaped shade and it was a real achievement to not get any blood stains on the fabric or the white lining — lampshade making involves a lot of pinning.'

Squint is an independent design company that produces and retails premium quality, bespoke, hand-crafted exuberant furniture and home accessories. It is the creation of Lisa Whatmough, who through her passion for textiles — and with a very British design sensibility — has created a world of richly decorative homewares that are a fusion of fashion and the decorative arts.

SQUINT LIMITED

www.squintlimited.com

Lisa originally trained as a sculptor and specialized in steel as a medium. She soon moved into painting, working with very strong fluorescent palettes: 'I can see an element of my early work in the designs Squint produces, a love both of pure colour, but how that works in a three-dimensional sense.'

Squint officially started in early 2005, with Lisa creating her first collection at home. Lisa has a passion for traditional Victorian and Edwardian shaped frames, and the company's signature style is the combination of multiple fabrics on a single piece. 'We see it as an exercise in addition of colour and pattern although it's always tagged as patchwork — I think of that more as the process than the end result.'

An off-site company supplies Squint with lampshades already covered with a neutral exterior lining. It's onto this exterior lining that Squint applies the fabric pieces. 'We work with fabric and glue and our process is a form of decoupage. The fabrics are glued up and then stretched over the shades in overlapping sections. It's an organic process in as much as creative decisions are made as we go along. It's impossible to predict how two contrasting colours will really look until you get going so we are editing and adding throughout to get the blend just so.'

RIGHT *Lisa particularly likes working with Japanese silk. 'The colours give off lovely tones of light through the prints, and Japanese design is exquisite.'*

ADVICE TO THE NOVICE MAKER

'It's great to make, but there is a difference between making and making a career, so if you want to earn a living from it consider your audience. If, however, you're making for yourself all bets are off and don't give any thought to what anyone else thinks, although as ever try and do it with a sense of quality.'

Miranda Law is the creative force behind Swee Mei Lampshades, based in West Sussex, England. All her lampshades have rigid frames, with drum shades her signature style but tapered shades growing in popularity. Her work is sold through Not On The High Street.

SWEE MEI LAMPSHADES

www.sweemei.co.uk

The name Swee Mei is the middle name of Miranda's daughter: 'My mother is Chinese Malaysian and she and my grandmother helped me to choose the name. Swee Mei means water jasmine. I'm Swee Kim (pretty gold) and my mum is Swee Ching (pretty teacup!).' Her Asian heritage is obvious from her lampshade designs and choice of materials. She has a passion for Japanese-style fabrics, with their bright colours and elaborate florals, coupled with a love of all things vintage.

Miranda loves the process, and still gets excited every time she rolls a lampshade and sees it become a three-dimensional object. She sources most of her fabrics online, and can spend hours scouring the internet for exotic and unusual examples. Initially, Miranda worked with mainly quilting and dressmaking cottons, but has since branched out into furnishing fabrics, linens and silks, which she says are a joy to work with. Her favourite and most important tool is her rotary cutter: 'The joys of a fresh blade are not to be underestimated!'

Swee Mei's lampshades were sold at first through Folksy online and craft fairs. Miranda has a dedicated Facebook business page, and Pinterest and Twitter accounts. She considers Facebook, 'An amazing way to reach an audience and get your work seen. I've found it to be friendly, supportive and I interact with lots of other lampshade makers on there. I could spend all day on Pinterest — such an overload of inspiration.'

ABOVE *Miranda chooses her fabrics very carefully. This one is made with House of Hackney's Palmeral, a cotton linen in white and green.*

Timorous Beasties was established in Glasgow, Scotland, in 1990 by Alistair McAuley and Paul Simmons, who met while studying textile design at Glasgow School of Art. Their work embodies a unique diversity of pattern, ranging from design that echoes a golden age of copperplate engraving, to examples of a distinctly edgy nature, a display of chic irreverence.

TIMOROUS BEASTIES

www.timorousbeasties.com

Timorous Beasties designs and prints all its own fabrics. 'Having the studio means we experiment with all sorts of things, we are very hands on in terms of production. We mix different inks, and varnishes, heat-sensitive inks, anything that is liquid and can be pushed through the mesh of a screen.'

Ali and Paul think of everything and see everything in terms of pattern and repeat, and the process involved in translating ideas into pattern and repeat. 'That's something that's constantly at the forefront of our thinking, to the point at which it becomes a mind-set; we like to make things that are aesthetically demanding, challenging even.'

They approach the printing process with the aesthetics of the lamp very much in mind. 'It's important to consider ink qualities and how that will play out in overlapping, shadowing, silhouettes, scales of detail. What is the best way to make the repeat; how will it play out directionally? Will the image on the lamp change all the way round? How will the pattern change under illumination, or in a state of darkness? Think about how the shade shape might govern the surface pattern. Then, think about what can make it different; how can one be economical with the pattern or material; and then, finally, sketch out some things, start designing.'

RIGHT *Ali and Paul (top) and members of the Timorous Beasties team busy screen printing in the studio (bottom).*

'Making is one of the most basic things about being human. Making is what elevates civilization!'

Zoë Darlington works from a small, but perfectly formed studio in Birmingham, England, where she makes strikingly beautiful lamps with the utmost respect for method and materials. Inspired by old heirlooms 'updated with a bold British wit', each lamp is designed to last a lifetime.

ZOË DARLINGTON

www.zoedarlington.co.uk

With a background in fine art and fashion, Zoë developed an interest in interiors and heritage craftsmanship. What began as a hobby turned into three years of further study and an obsession with the lost art of lampshade making before Zoë launched her business in 2011. She also runs the very popular Shade School, in which she shares her passion for the fine craft of traditional lampshade making.

Zoë's lamp bases are hand-turned from the finest timbers by traditional English artisans. The shades are designed and made personally by Zoë. Sculptural frames are welded locally; patterns are expertly chalked and hand-cut; fabrics and trims are meticulously hand-stitched to frames. The combination of traditional form and practice, and unexpected colour and pattern, creates something utterly contemporary, quintessentially British and, above all, beautiful.

Zoë says of her lamp-making philosophy: 'I strive to create the finest shades possible using heritage techniques and to give my clients something so perfect that it elevates their space. Every lamp is handmade in Britain using techniques unchanged for generations. Process is incredibly important to me. It's very important to me to retain this element of control over my practice and I don't ever want to lose touch with the physicality of making.'

RIGHT *Zoë in her studio. Her time in fashion taught her how fabrics work and fuelled her love for colour and print.*

ADVICE FOR THE NOVICE MAKER
'Start with a small project so you don't feel overwhelmed or frustrated, and don't be surprised that it takes a long time to make; and wear a thimble for all that hand stitching, and make sure you have a supply of plasters! I'd also recommend taking a course. You can't beat one-to-one teaching in a fun environment surrounded by like-minded people.'

LIGHTBOX

Mols & Tati-Lois

Lampara

Abigail Ahern

Swee Mei Lampshades

Folly & Glee

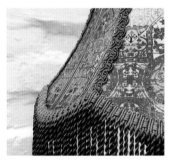

Mols & Tati-Lois

Mols & Tati-Lois

Zoë Darlington

Timorous Beasties

Made by Sally Whiting

Mols & Tati-Lois

Mineheart

Squint Limited

Boris Design Studio

Squint Limited

Mols & Tati-Lois

Zoë Darlington

BeauVamp

GLOSSARY

Accent lighting Used to highlight and draw attention to specific areas or objects within a room.

Ambient lighting This is the background light that you find in pretty much every room in a home. Makes a space feel cosy.

Bias The bias is at 45 degrees to the vertical warp and horizontal weft threads of a fabric.

Bias cut To cut fabric in a way so that the grain runs diagonally, rather than straight up and down.

Bold thread A strong thread ideal for lampshade making.

Boomerang An adaptor that fits on to the gimbal to convert the fitting from the standard North American and European ES fitting (27mm diameter) to the standard British fitting (22mm diameter).

Carrier These support a duplex fitting on a standard lamp base and come in different sizes.

Cross grain This runs perpendicular to the selvedge and parallel to the weft threads. Usually has more stretch than the straight grain.

Decorative lighting This type of lighting is more of a statement than a source of light, and usually serves little purpose other than to look beautiful.

Decoupage The art of decorating an object by gluing paper or fabric on to it. Layers are often sealed using varnish.

Diffuser Diffuses light to create a soft light.

Duplex A duplex fitting is a large 110mm fitting and is usually found on large standard lamp frames.

Face down This refers to fabric. When a fabric is face down it is right side down/wrong side up. In other words it means the pattern side is face down.

Face up This refers to fabric. When a fabric is face up it is right side up/wrong side down. In other words it means the pattern side is face up.

Fat Quarter (FQ) A quarter of a yard of fabric usually measuring 18in x 22in (46 x 56cm) as opposed to a regular quarter yard which measures 9in x 44in (23 x 112cm).

Fitting The fitting of a frame is the part that attaches to the light source, regardless of whether it is a lamp base or a pendant fitting.

Gallery The pelmet-like panels that run around the bottom of a frame to give an extra layer of panels.

Gimbal Attaches the fitting to the frame. A reversible gimbal can change a fitting from a pendant shade to a table shade.

Inbetweens Short, sturdy needles, ideal for lampshade making as they do not snap as easily as regular dressmaking needles.

Lills Also known as sequin pins, these are ideal for pinning fabric to your frame. Lills are shorter than regular dressmaking pins.

Right side The 'pattern' side of a fabric, so the side that you will want facing out once you have finished your lampshade.

Spider This transforms a duplex fitting into a pendant fitting.

Straight grain Runs parallel to the warp threads and the selvedge. Typically has less stretch than the cross grain.

Streetly stitch Traditional lampshade-making locking stitch. A combination of a running stitch and a back stitch.

Strut Sometimes referred to as arm or stave, this is the vertical coated metal pole joining top and bottom ring together.

Task lighting A type of lighting that makes carrying out tasks easier. Tends to be directional without a great deal of diffusion. Examples include desk lighting, bathroom lighting over a mirror, and light fittings found in kitchens.

Warp The threads that run vertically on a frame or loom.

Weft The threads that run horizontally on a frame or loom.

Wrong side The 'reverse' side of a fabric, so the side that you will want facing inwards once you have finished your lampshade.

RESOURCES

Frames, kits, flexes and other supplies
www.hobbycraft.co.uk
www.needcraft.co.uk
www.ebay.co.uk/usr/frameman1
www.ebay.com
www.fredaldous.co.uk
www.urbancottageindustries.com
www.dowsingandreynolds.com/
www.premierlampshades.co.uk/
www.fireproofspray.co.uk
www.fireprotectiononline.co.uk/
fire-retardant-spray.html
www.fireretardantspray.co.uk
www.lampshop.com
www.screwfix.com
www.toolstation.com

Vintage and pre-loved finds (frames, bases, fabrics)
www.1stdibs.com
www.iacf.co.uk/ardingly
www.ebay.com
www.alfiesantiques.com
www.preloved.co.uk
www.salvo.co.uk
www.atomica.me.uk
www.sunburyantiques.com
www.theoldcinema.co.uk
www.donnaflower.com
www.decorativecollective.com
www.retrouvius.com

Fabrics and trims
www.vvrouleaux.com
www.macculloch-wallis.co.uk
www.frumble.co.uk
www.plushaddict.co.uk
www.raystitch.co.uk
www.michaelmillerfabrics.com
www.robertkaufman.com
www.ahfabrics.com
www.amybutlerdesign.com
www.liberty.co.uk
www.conran.com
www.designersguild.com

www.harlequin.uk.com
www.manuelcanovas.com
www.osborneandlittle.com
www.ninacampbell.com
www.zoffany.com
www.zimmer-rohde.com
www.sander-son.co.uk
www.fabric.com
www.sisboom.com
http://theoldhaberdashery.com
www.spoonflower.com
www.houseofhackney.com
www.celiabirtwell.com
www.bazaarshop.co.uk
www.williamgee.co.uk
thefabricshophoramltd.co.uk
www.joelandsonfabrics.com
www.myfabrics.co.uk
www.bltrimmings.com
http://merchantandmills.com

Websites
www.abigailahern.com
www.beauvamp.com
www.borisdesignstudio.com
http://follyandglee.bigcartel.com
www.homeofrockville.co.uk
www.lampara.co.uk
www.facebook.com/
madebysallywhiting
www.mineheart.com
www.squintlimited.com
www.sweemei.co.uk
www.timorousbeasties.com
www.zoedarlington.co.uk
www.shadezofmichelle.com
www.jonathanadler.com
www.mintshop.co.uk
www.caravanstyle.com
www.johnderian.com
www.pedlars.co.uk
www.ptolemymann.com
www.tomdixon.net/uk
www.anakras.com
www.rockettstgeorge.co.uk
www.lauraoakes.co.uk

https://uk.pinterest.com/natipricecab
www.trendland.com
http://designtaxi.com
www.bonstudio.co.uk
www.molsandtati-lois.com

Blogs
decor8blog.com
decorenvy.co.uk
em.elledecoration.se
www.brightbazaarblog.com
www.sfgirlbybay.com
http://confessionsofadesigngeek.com
www.designspongeonline.com
www.apartmenttherapy.com
www.theartofdoingstuff.com
www.design-milk.com

Magazines
Making:
www.makingmagazine.com
Reloved:
www.relovedmag.co.uk
Selvedge:
www.selvedge.org
Mollie Makes:
www.molliemakes.com

Apps
Magpie by Conran: Create
moodboards you can print.
My Pantone: Create colour palettes
and share them with others; find
a colour match from a photograph.

Workshops and courses
www.thegoodlifecentre.co.uk
www.molsandtati-lois.com
www.zoedarlington.co.uk
www.facebook.com/MolsTatiLois
www.mojidesigns.com
www.follyandglee.co.uk

Selling your products
Folksy
Etsy

ACKNOWLEDGEMENTS

Thank you to Jonathan Bailey, Publisher at GMC Publications Ltd., for his unequivocal belief in me and what I wanted to achieve. Big thanks to Dominique Page, my editor, for championing this project wholeheartedly. Thanks, too, to the whole team at GMC Publications Ltd. and to Jason Hook.

A very big thank you to all the fantastically talented creatives featured in this book, who gave freely of their time, words and pictures, and without whom this project would not have come to fruition. We salute you Abigail Ahern, Alice Moylan of BeauVamp, Anna Karlsson and Katarina Ivarsson of Boris Design Studio, Polly Kettley and Amelia Bur of Folly & Glee, Charlotte Elfdahl of Rockville, Diane Wilson of Lampara, Sally Whiting of Made by Sally Whiting, Brendan Young and Vanessa Battaglia of Mineheart, Lisa Whatmough of Squint Limited, Miranda Law of Swee Mei Lampshades, Hannah Mitchell, Paul Simmons and Ali McAuley of Timorous Beasties, Zoë Darlington, and Michelle Tomlinson of Shadez of Michelle.

And an additional huge thank you to Chris Gatcum for all his wonderful photography in this book. He went over and above the call of duty. And to Kate Haynes for such superb design. Kate always manages to sprinkle some magic on to a project and she really has pulled out all the stops on this book. It looks truly beautiful and is even more incredible than I could ever have imagined. A special thank you to Jo Hall of Bazaar for many of the fabulous trimmings and fabrics featured in this book.

This book is dedicated to my amazing Dad, James Henry Price, who sadly is no longer with us, but who I know would have been chuffed to bits to see me write a book of my own after nearly 20 years of editing other people's words.

To my handsome, clever, patient partner Chris for all his support, belief and enthusiasm, a big thank you. He bought me my first, second and third sewing machine all in the space of a few months and encouraged me to do courses. And to our two beautiful and funny daughters, Tatiana and Georgia-Mae, for endless sweet cuddles and kisses, and making me laugh a lot. To my wonderful Mum, Susana Price, I love you. My brilliant sisters, Cal, Shedgie and Annie, and all my nieces, nephews and brothers-in-law, thank you for always believing in me and buoying me up through good and bad times. To my 'parents-in-law', Jeff and Pat. Collectively you are the best family ever. To Bibbi and Sarah, you are the best friends a girl could ever have or need. A huge thank you for just being you. I love you both heaps.

Thank you to my very wonderful work buddies, who are so much more than that – Zara, Frank, Rachel, Roly, Julie and Adam. And thank you to all the frankly amazing people who I have had the delight of crossing paths with over recent years, either physically or virtually – you have all been an inspiration.

'Light can be gentle, dangerous, dreamlike, bare, living, dead, misty, clear, hot, dark, violet, springlike, falling, straight, sensual, limited, poisonous, calm and soft.'

SVEN NYKVIST

Picture credits

All images © Chris Gatcum unless indicated otherwise.

p8: Victorian lampshade illustration: Courtesy iStock / © duncan1890; Tiffany lampshade: iStock photo © mandj98; 3 x contemporary turn-of-the century 1900 lampshades: Courtesy of Michelle Tomlinson, Shadez of Michelle, www.shadezofmichelle.com.

p9: Marcel Wanders ANDAZ hotel lighting © frans lemmens / Alamy; Ingo Maurer Zettel'z 5 © Borislav Dopudja / Alamy.

p51: Get Inspired/Swee Mei Lampshades courtesy of Miranda Law, Swee Mei Lampshades.

p53: Made by Sally Whiting lifestyle shot courtesy of Made by Sally Whiting www.facebook.com/madebysallywhiting / photograph © Jayne Sacco, Sacco and Sacco Photography www.saccophotography.co.uk.

p57: Get Inspired image courtesy of Made by Sally Whiting www.facebook.com/madebysallywhiting / photograph © Jayne Sacco, Sacco and Sacco Photography www.saccophotography.co.uk

p71: Get Inspired Lampara image courtesy of Diane Wilson, Lampara / photograph by Michelle Rosaus; Get Inspired Timorous Beasties image courtesy of Timorous Beasties.

p87: Get Inspired Rockville image courtesy of Charlotte Elfdahl, Rockville / photograph by Fredrik Elfdahl; Get Inspired Zoë Darlington image courtesy of Zoë Darlington www.zoedarlington.co.uk / photograph by Natalie Dinham www.nataliedinham.com.

p101: Get Inspired Boris image © 2015 Boris Design Studio Ltd.

p113: Get Inspired BeauVamp image courtesy of BeauVamp / photograph by Claire Sutton Images www.clairesuttonimages.com; Get Inspired Zoë Darlington image courtesy of Zoë Darlington / photograph by UK Packshot www.ukpackshot.com.

p119: Get Inspired Squint image courtesy of Squint Limited.

p125: Get Inspired BeauVamp image courtesy of BeauVamp.

p157: Get Inspired Abigail Ahern image courtesy of Abigail Ahern; Get Inspired Mineheart image courtesy of Mineheart www.mineheart.com.

p158: clockwise from top left: courtesy of Rockville / photograph by Fredrik Elfdahl; courtesy of Diane Wilson, Lampara / photograph by Michelle Rosaus; courtesy of Mineheart www.mineheart.com; courtesy of Squint Limited; courtesy of Timorous Beasties; courtesy of Made by Sally Whiting www.facebook.com/madebysallywhiting / photograph © Jayne Sacco, Sacco and Sacco Photography www.saccophotography.co.uk; courtesy of Zoë Darlington www.zoedarlington.co.uk / photograph by UK Packshot www.ukpackshot.com; courtesy of Abigail Ahern; courtesy of Miranda Law, Swee Mei Lampshades; photograph © 2015 Boris Design Studio Ltd.; courtesy of BeauVamp; courtesy of Folly & Glee, The Long Barn Studios, Upper Lodge, Sussex www.upperlodgesussex.com.

pp160-161: all images courtesy of Abigail Ahern.

p162: courtesy of BeauVamp / photograph by Claire Sutton Images www.clairesuttonimages.com.

p163: top row, left: courtesy of BeauVamp / photograph by Claire Sutton Images www.clairesuttonimages.com; top row, centre: courtesy of BeauVamp; top row, right: courtesy of BeauVamp / photograph by Bon Studio www.bonstudio.co.uk; second row, left: courtesy of BeauVamp / photograph by Claire Sutton Images www.clairesuttonimages.com; second row, centre: courtesy of BeauVamp; third row, left: courtesy of BeauVamp / photograph by Claire Sutton Images www.clairesuttonimages.com; third row, middle left: courtesy of BeauVamp; third row, middle right and right: courtesy of BeauVamp / photograph by Claire Sutton Images www.clairesuttonimages.com; bottom row, left: courtesy of BeauVamp / photograph by Bon Studio www.bonstudio.co.uk; bottom row, right: courtesy of BeauVamp.

pp164–165: photographs © 2015 Boris Design Studio Ltd.

p167: top row, far right: courtesy of Folly & Glee; second row, middle: courtesy of Folly & Glee; third row, first image: courtesy of Folly & Glee; bottom row, left: courtesy of Folly & Glee, The Long Barn Studios, Upper Lodge, Sussex www.upperlodgesussex.com.

p168: courtesy of Diane Wilson, Lampara / photograph by Michelle Rosaus.

p169: portrait photography by Rogerio Fernandes; all other images courtesy of Diane Wilson, Lampara / photograph by Michelle Rosaus.

pp170–171: courtesy of Made by Sally Whiting www.facebook.com/madebysallywhiting / photograph © Jayne Sacco, Sacco and Sacco Photography www.saccophotography.co.uk.

pp172–173: courtesy of Mineheart www.mineheart.com.

p175: top row, left: photograph © David Merewether www.davidmerewether.co.uk; top row, middle: photograph © Fredrik Elfdahl; top row, right: photograph © Guy Montagu-Pollock; second row, left: photograph © Fredrik Elfdahl; second row, middle: photograph © Peter Pilon; second row, right: photograph © Fredrik Elfdahl; third row, left: photograph © David Merewether www.davidmerewether.co.uk; third row, middle: photograph © Fredrik Elfdahl; third row, right: photograph © David Merewether www.davidmerewether.co.uk; bottom row, left: photograph © Fredrik Elfdahl; bottom row, centre: photograph © Guy Montagu-Pollock; bottom row, right: photograph © Fredrik Elfdahl

p176: courtesy of Squint Limited.

p177: portrait photograph by Astrid Grosser; all other images courtesy of Squint Limited.

p178: courtesy of Miranda Law, Swee Mei Lampshades.

p179: courtesy of Miranda Law, Swee Mei Lampshades; bottom row, right: photograph by Dan Law.

p180–181: courtesy of Timorous Beasties.

p182: courtesy of Zoë Darlington www.zoedarlington.co.uk.

p183: top row, left and centre: courtesy of Zoë Darlington www.zoedarlington.co.uk / photograph by Natalie Dinham www.nataliedinham.com; top row, right: courtesy of Zoë Darlington www.zoedarlington.co.uk / photograph by UK Packshot www.ukpackshot.com; second row, left: courtesy of Zoë Darlington www.zoedarlington.co.uk / photograph by UK Packshot www.ukpackshot.com; second row, centre and right: courtesy of Zoë Darlington www.zoedarlington.co.uk / photograph by Natalie Dinham www.nataliedinham.com; third row, left and centre: courtesy of Zoë Darlington www.zoedarlington.co.uk / photograph by Natalie Dinham www.nataliedinham.com; third row, right: courtesy of Zoë Darlington www.zoedarlington.co.uk / photograph by UK Packshot www.ukpackshot.com; fourth row, left: courtesy of Zoë Darlington www.zoedarlington.co.uk / photograph by Natalie Dinham www.nataliedinham.com; fourth row, right: courtesy of Zoë Darlington www.zoedarlington.co.uk.

p184: top row, centre: courtesy of Diane Wilson, Lampara / photograph by Michelle Rosaus; top row, right: courtesy of Abigail Ahern; second row, left: courtesy of Miranda Law, Swee Mei Lampshades; second row, centre: courtesy of Folly & Glee, The Long Barn Studios, Upper Lodge, Sussex www.upperlodgesussex.com; bottom row, centre: courtesy of Zoë Darlington www.zoedarlington.co.uk / photograph by UK Packshot www.ukpackshot.com; bottom row, right: courtesy of Timorous Beasties

p185: top row, left: courtesy of Made by Sally Whiting www.facebook.com/madebysallywhiting / photograph © Jayne Sacco, Sacco and Sacco Photography www.saccophotography.co.uk; top row, right: courtesy of Mineheart www.mineheart.com; second row, left: courtesy of Squint Limited; second row, centre: photographs © 2015 Boris Design Studio Ltd.; second row, right: Courtesy of Squint Limited; bottom row, centre: courtesy of Zoë Darlington www.zoedarlington.co.uk / photograph by UK Packshot www.ukpackshot.com; bottom row, right: courtesy of BeauVamp / photograph by Claire Sutton Images www.clairesuttonimages.com.

INDEX

To place an order, or to request a catalogue, contact:
GMC Publications Ltd
Castle Place, 166 High Street, Lewes, East Sussex, BN7 1XU
United Kingdom
+44 (0)1273 488005
www.gmcbooks.com